NATIONAL GEOGRAPHIC LEARNING | CENGAGE Learning

WORKBOOK 4

TIME ZONES

W0018786

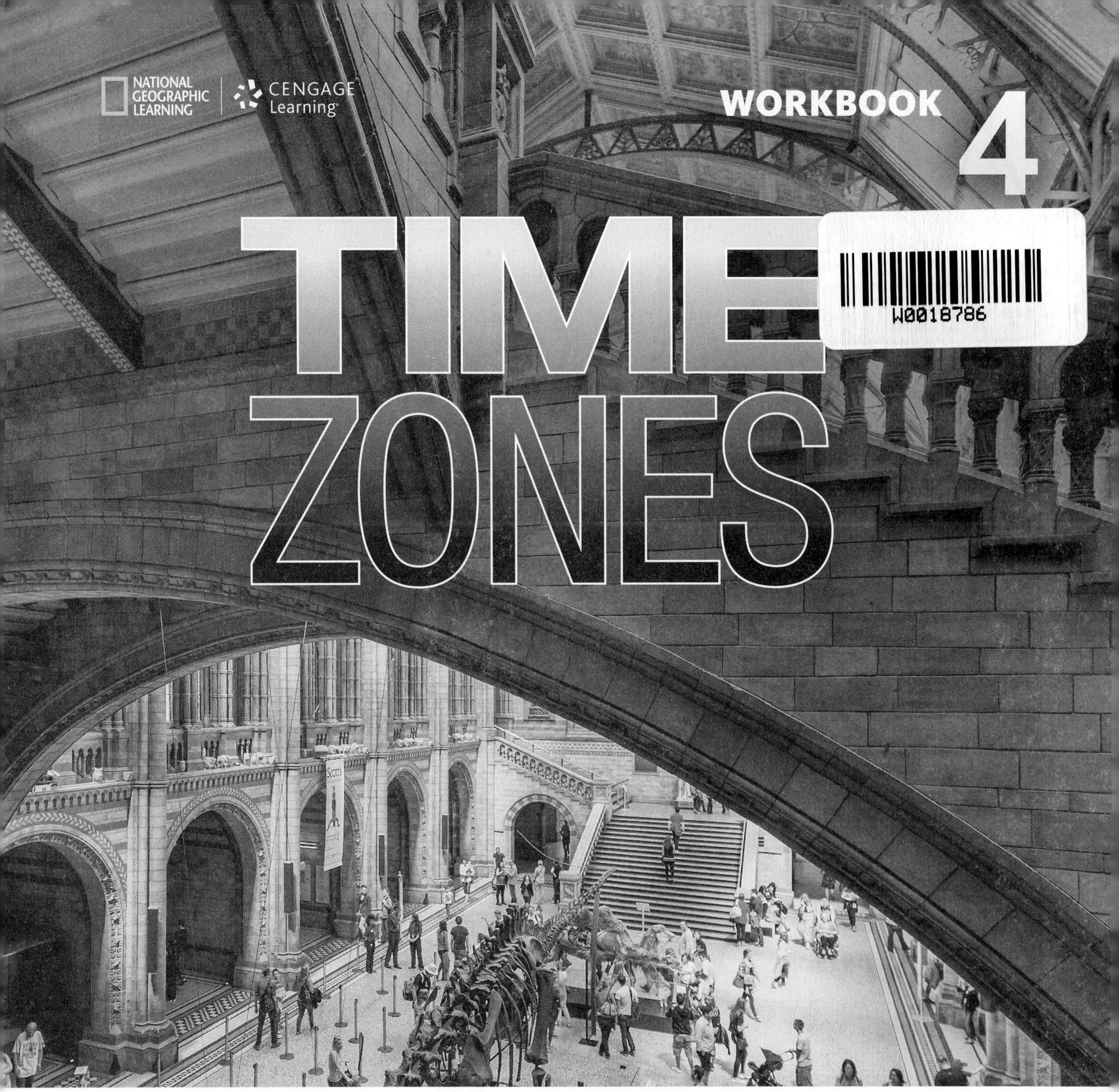

David Bohlke

SECOND EDITION

NATIONAL GEOGRAPHIC LEARNING | CENGAGE Learning

Australia • Brazil • Japan • Korea • Mexico • Singapore • Spain • United Kingdom • United States

Time Zones Workbook 4
Second Edition

David Bohlke

Publisher: Andrew Robinson

Senior Development Editor: Derek Mackrell

Associate Development Editors:
Michelle Harris, Melissa Pang

Director of Global Marketing: Ian Martin

Product Marketing Manager: Anders Bylund

Media Researcher: Leila Hishmeh

Senior Director of Production:
Michael Burggren

Senior Content Project Manager:
Tan Jin Hock

Manufacturing Planner:
Mary Beth Hennebury

Compositor: Cenveo Publisher Services

Cover/Text Design: Creative Director:
Christopher Roy, Art Director: Scott Baker,
Senior Designer: Michael Rosenquest

Cover Photo: Natural History Museum,
London, England: Massimo Borchi/Atlantide
Phototravel/Corbis

ISBN-13: 978-1-305-25995-9

National Geographic Learning
20 Channel Center Street
Boston, MA 02210
USA

Cengage Learning is a leading provider of customized learning solutions with employees residing in nearly 40 different countries and sales in more than 125 countries around the world. Find your local representative at:
www.cengage.com

Cengage Learning products are represented in Canada by Nelson Education, Ltd.

Visit National Geographic Learning online at **NGL.Cengage.com**

Visit our corporate website at **www.cengage.com**

Printed in the United States of America
Print Number: 03   Print Year: 2016

Contents

I LOVE MAKING JEWELRY!

Vocabulary Focus

A **Match.** Where would you usually do these activities? Join the activities to the places.

1. swimming ○   ○ a. on a mountain

2. performing ○   ○ b. in a kitchen

3. baking ○   ○ c. in a pool

4. exercising ○   ○ d. in a gym

5. skiing ○   ○ e. on a stage

B **Read the descriptions.** Then complete the sentences using the phrases in the box.

> ~~building models~~   making jewelry   playing the guitar   reading comic books
> doing puzzles   playing board games   ~~playing sports~~   writing a blog

1. Luke loves playing basketball and hopes to join the school team one day. He also has a large collection of airplanes he has built over the years.

   Luke loves _playing sports and building models_ .

2. Tanya likes writing online about her favorite musicians and singers. She also plays an instrument in a band called The Parker Sisters.

   Tanya likes _____ .

3. Michiko enjoys making bracelets and necklaces in her free time. She is also very good at both checkers and backgammon.

   Michiko enjoys _____ .

4. Rick enjoys reading graphic novels such as *X-Men*. In his free time, he relaxes by doing crosswords and word searches.

   Rick enjoys _____ .

Conversation

Complete the conversation. Put the sentences in the correct order.
IN CLASS Practice with a partner.

a. __1__ Wow! You're really good at playing the guitar.

b. _____ I like playing hockey, but I love watching soccer on TV. I think it's the most exciting sport to watch.

c. _____ Thanks! Do you play any instruments?

d. _____ Me, too! I never miss a match when my favorite team is playing.

e. _____ Oh? What sports do you like?

f. _____ No, I don't. I'm not very musical, I guess. I prefer playing sports.

Language Focus

A **Correct one mistake in each sentence.**

1. I don't like playing video games, but I enjoy play board games.

2. Celia loves to sing, but perform in front of people makes her nervous.

3. Jan likes cook, but she doesn't like to bake at all.

4. I don't like running in a gym. I prefer jog outdoors.

5. I don't like hip-hop music. In fact, I wouldn't stand it.

B **Put the words in the correct order to form questions.** Then complete the answers.

1. A: Mike / like / Does / playing golf _Does Mike like playing golf?_____

   B: No, he can't _stand_____ it.

2. A: What / doing / Hal and Linda / do / enjoy _____

   B: They enjoy _____ puzzles.

3. A: hiking / favorite / Pam's / activity / Is _____

   B: _____, she loves it!

4. A: cooking / like / Do / you _____

   B: No, I don't really _____ cooking.

5. A: Charles / like / does / doing / What _____

   B: He likes _____ video games.

The Real World

Put down that phone! More and more young people today are beginning to tire of technology, and have been turning to the hobbies of their parents—and even grandparents! It seems that what was once old-fashioned is now hip. Millennials—those born between 1980 and 2000—seem to have found a new interest in making things with their own hands. This DIY culture has resulted in hobbies like canning, soap making, and beekeeping becoming more popular among city residents.

These hobbies are cheap, don't require a lot of space, and are easy to do! Canning is a way of making food last longer. It is a great way to prepare homemade jams, jellies, and pickles for family and friends. Those who enjoy soap making make soaps that are healthy for the skin and that don't contain harmful chemicals. As for beekeeping, it has many benefits besides providing honey. Beeswax can be used to make candles, soaps, and wood polish.

This DIY culture among millennials can be a way for some to set themselves apart from others. For other millennials, it may remind them of simpler times. Or maybe, it's the sense of achievement people can get from these DIY hobbies.

A **Read the article.** What is the best title for this article?

a. What Is a Millennial?　　　b. Old Is New Again　　　c. Hobbies that Cost Nothing

B **Answer the questions.** Circle the correct answers.

1. The word "hip" could be replaced with the word _____ .

　　a. outdated　　　　　　b. trendy　　　　　　c. fancy

2. DIY stands for _____ .

　　a. Doing It Young　　　b. Do It Yearly　　　c. Do It Yourself

3. Which of the following hobbies is NOT similar to the ones in the article?

　　a. playing soccer　　　b. knitting　　　c. making furniture

Reading

A **Skim the article.** What is the purpose of the article?

    a. to describe the most popular activities among teens

    b. to show trends in leisure-time use over the years

    c. to compare leisure-time use between two age groups

LEISURE TIME **SURVEY**

Everyone would like to have more free time. But what do people do in their free time? The U.S. Bureau of Labor Statistics conducted a survey to ask people of different age groups this question. The chart below compares the results for two groups: millennials and retirees (people above 60 years old). When it comes to free time, what do these two groups have in common? According to the survey results, not much.

The biggest contrast between these two groups is the amount of reading that they do for leisure. Millennials spend very little time reading compared to retirees. Retirees also spend twice as much time as working adults watching TV. Interestingly, the survey showed that both groups spent the same amount of time doing sports and exercise.

Retirees fill their time with activities to keep themselves occupied. Millennials use their free time to relax after a hard day's work. Millennials probably spend much more time socializing and communicating to expand their circle of friends, while retirees most likely use the time to keep in touch with old friends.

Leisure time is important for everyone. It allows us to rest from the day-to-day stresses of work, school, and other commitments. And although the survey did not ask this, it is likely that we all would like to have more time for leisure than we do now.

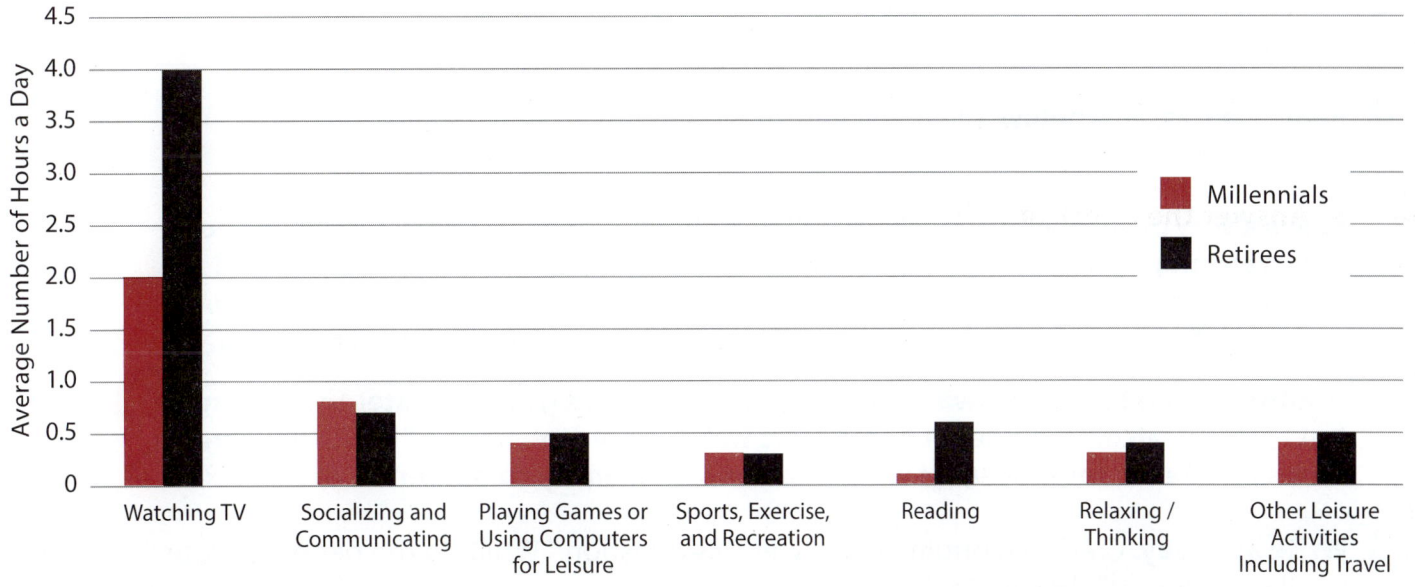

Leisure Hours Spent by Millennials and Retirees

B **Read the article and look at the graph.** Circle **T** for True or **F** for False.

1. Millennials and retirees spend their leisure time in very similar ways.	**T**	**F**
2. Both groups spend most of their free time watching TV.	**T**	**F**
3. Both groups spend fewer than 30 minutes every day on socializing.	**T**	**F**
4. Millennials spend the least amount of their free time reading.	**T**	**F**
5. Retirees spend the least amount of their free time using the computer for leisure.	**T**	**F**

C **Why do you think both groups spend so little time doing sports and exercise?** **IN CLASS** Talk with a partner.

Writing

WRITING TIP **Creating an outline**

Use an outline to help you organize your ideas before you begin writing. The outline shows your main ideas and supporting details. As you begin writing, you can omit or add information.

What I Like Doing

Sports
- watching soccer: favorite players, World Cup, . . .
- playing tennis: lessons, future goals, . . .

Watching movies
- at the movie theater
- at home: watch on TV, rent DVDs, online . . .

Traveling

A **Read the passage below.** Circle the information in the outline that appears in the passage.

I have a very busy schedule at school, so I don't have a lot of free time. But when I do, I love watching soccer. Two of my favorite players are Lionel Messi and Gareth Bale. I watch soccer all the time, and especially love watching World Cup matches. I play sports, too. I take tennis lessons twice a week and hope to be on the school team next year.

Another interest of mine is watching movies. I sometimes go to a theater to see a movie, but I prefer watching movies at home. I like watching old movies on TV with my parents. When my friends come over, we watch movies online on my computer.

B **Write an essay.** Create an outline to answer this question: "What do the people in your family like doing?" Then write a short essay.

HOW LONG HAVE YOU BEEN PLAYING **CRICKET?**

Vocabulary Focus

A **Write.** Complete the crossword puzzle.

Across

2.
4.
8.
9.
10.
11.

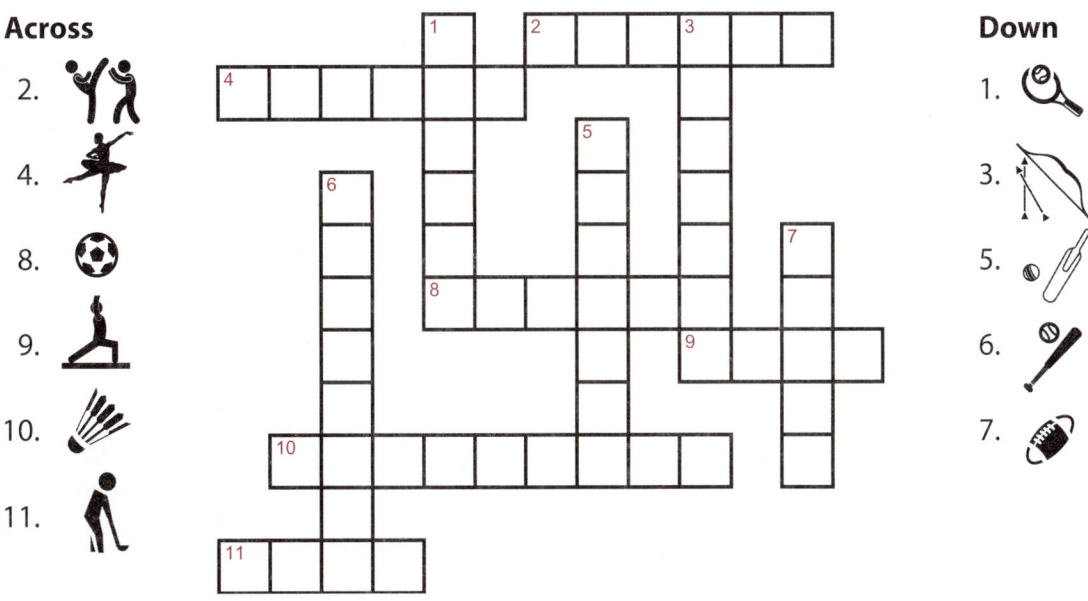

Down

1.
3.
5.
6.
7.

B **Complete the chart.** Use the words in **A**.

do + _____	play + _____
archery	badminton

C **Circle your answers.** Which activities in **B** can you do alone?

Conversation

Complete the conversation. Use the correct forms of the words in the box.

IN CLASS Practice with a partner.

> save   tutor   meet   work   not answer

Jan: Hey, Karl! I haven't seen you in a while! What are you doing here?

Karl: Hi, Jan! How are you? I was supposed to (1) _____ my friend Brian here. I guess he's running late.

Jan: Why don't you try calling him?

Karl: I did, but he (2) _____ his phone. I'll call him again if he's not here soon.

Jan: What are you guys going to do?

Karl: We're going to a baseball game. The Tigers have been playing well lately, so it should be a good game. What's new with you?

Jan: Not much. I (3) _____ here at Café Central since June. I'm trying to (4) _____ money for college.

Karl: Oh, yeah? I have a job, too. I (5) _____ some kids in English for the past couple of months.

Language Focus

Complete the questions and answers. Use the correct forms of the words in parentheses. Add *for* or *since* where necessary.

IN CLASS Practice with a partner.

1. A: How long has Andy _____? (**go to the gym**)
   B: He _____. (**two years**)

2. A: Has Ana _____? (**take tennis lessons / a long time**)
   B: Yes, she _____. (**middle school**)

3. A: How long _____? (**rain**)
   B: It _____. (**about an hour**)

4. A: Why _____? (**you / not return my calls / recently**)
   B: Sorry, but I _____. (**study really hard / lately**)

5. A: How long _____? (**you / watching TV**)
   B: I _____. (**8:30**)

The Real World

A **Scan the article.** What is the best title for the article?

a. The History of Wrestling   b. Modern Wrestling   c. The Olympic Games

Wrestling is a very old sport. It has been an Olympic sport since 708 B.C. Archaeological evidence shows paintings of wrestlers on tombs in Egypt, some from as early as 2500 B.C. Ancient cave paintings in France and Iraq—some over 15,000 years old—show wrestlers in action. The holds shown in these paintings are remarkably similar to the holds wrestlers use today.

Wrestling became very popular in France, Japan, and England during the Middle Ages (A.D. 500–A.D. 1500), and royal families often sponsored the sport. When settlers from England arrived in the Americas, they brought wrestling with them, and found that the Native American tribes also enjoyed wrestling. The sport grew in the United States, becoming popular at state fairs.

To this day, wrestling remains popular worldwide. It is the national sport in several countries, including Mongolia, Iran, and Turkey. Wrestling was also a main sporting event at the first modern Olympic Games in 1896, and continues to draw crowds of fans.

B **Read the article.** Circle the correct answers.

1. Wrestling has been an Olympic sport since ____ .

   a. 2500 B.C.   b. 708 B.C.   c. 1896

2. Why are the cave paintings in France and Iraq remarkable?

   a. They show Native Americans wrestling.

   b. They provide evidence that royal families sponsored the sport.

   c. They show that wrestling hasn't changed much over the years.

3. The word "sponsored" means ____ .

   a. supported   b. disliked   c. watched

Reading

A **Skim the article.** The article is about Navarro's work as a surfer and _____.

a. conservationist   b. politician   c. journalist

WAVES OF **CHANGE**

"In my dreams, I'd never thought a wave could be that perfect," says Chilean surfer Ramon Navarro of the wave he surfed in Fiji in June 2012. The wave was a perfect, curling tube big enough to drive a truck through. He surfed it so beautifully that many surfers have called it the best tube ride ever.

Navarro came from a family of fishermen, and this had a big influence on him. He has been surfing since he was 12. As a child, his parents taught him to care about the ocean; he says it was one of the first things he knew about. Today, he is one of the best big-wave surfers in the world.

Navarro is passionate about surfing, but he is also actively involved in protecting the ocean around his birthplace of Punta de Lobos. When he learned that a sewage pipe was going to release untreated waste into the bay of his hometown, he decided to do something about it. He reached out to local politicians and international organizations. He also organized surfers and locals to speak against it. His efforts successfully prevented water pollution in the area.

Navarro has also been working with the Chilean government and conservation groups to turn the stretch of coast in his hometown into a national park. Industrial activities can change the landscape and the waves. The population of Chile's Patagonia region sees conservation as a way to bring in tourism. It's also the way Navarro feels he can protect his own corner of Chile.

"The Chilean people have been really involved in the environmental movement," says Navarro. "If we protect our land, take care of our country, we will have a better standard of living."

B **Read the article.** Circle the correct answers.

1. Main Idea Navarro is working to get people to _____.

    a. take up surfing   b. protect the ocean   c. practice safe fishing techniques

2. Vocabulary What's another word for "passionate"?

    a. enthusiastic   b. knowledgeable   c. confident

3. **Detail** Which of the following actions did Navarro take to prevent water pollution in his hometown?

   a. He created a website.

   b. He built a special water filter.

   c. He brought the matter to the government's attention.

4. **Inference** Which of the following groups of people is most likely to object to Navarro's proposal for a national park?

   a. local residents   b. the Chilean government   c. factory owners

Writing

WRITING TIP **Combining sentences**

To avoid too many short sentences and to make your writing more natural, combine sentences. You can join ideas together using words like **and**, **but**, **or**, and **so**.

I've been playing rugby for years, and I hope to continue playing it.

I like playing basketball, but I don't like playing baseball.

I may go to the game on Friday, or I may watch it on TV.

I have my ballet class in the morning, so I can't stay out late tonight.

A   **Read the email.** Underline the combined sentences. Then write a reply.

> To: diego104@mailtoyou.com
>
> Subject: Pen pals?
> _____
>
> Hi!
>
> My name is Alison, and I'm a student at Lincoln High School. My teacher says our classes are going to write emails to each other this year. Cool!
>
> I love martial arts. My favorite is taekwondo. I've been doing it for three years, and I have a yellow belt. I also like playing basketball, but I'm not very good at it. How about you? Do you play sports or do any martial arts?
>
> Well, it's late now, so I'm going to bed. Hope to hear from you soon!
>
> Alison

B   **Rewrite your email.** Find places to join sentences.
IN CLASS Read your reply to a partner.

YOU COULD ASK FOR ADVICE.

Vocabulary Focus

A **Complete the sentences.** Use the phrases in the box. One is extra.

> buy a new one   don't lend things   go to the library
>
> join a study group   get it repaired   tell your teacher

TIPS FOR NEW STUDENTS

Visit our computer center.

If you don't have a computer, you can (1) _____ . There are special
tables with computers you can use. If you would like to (2) _____ ,
you can come to us and we'll recommend some models to suit your budget. If you
have problems with your own computer, our computer support center can help
you (3) _____ .

Study hard!

Do you enjoy studying with others? You could (4) _____ . Many of
our students say they like the extra support they get from working with others. If
you need more help, speak to our tutors. They would love to help you!

Talk to someone.

If you have a problem with a classmate, we suggest you (5) _____ .
Our staff can help solve a variety of problems.

B **Match the problems to the advice.**

1. It's hard to learn new vocabulary.   O   O   a. Ask her to buy you a new one.

2. My phone broke.   O   O   b. I wouldn't say anything.

3. I want to tell my sister she's gained weight.   O   O   c. You could try getting it repaired.

4. My friend lost the book I lent her.   O   O   d. You should apologize.

5. I told my mother her jacket looked ugly.   O   O   e. Why don't you try using flashcards?

Conversation

Complete the conversation. Put the words in the correct order.

IN CLASS Practice with a partner.

Wes: You look upset, Greg. 1. (**OK / everything / Is**) _____?

Greg: 2. (**jacket / my brother's / borrowed / I / yesterday**) _____
_____ , and I spilled tomato juice all over it.

Wes: Oh, no! 3. (**tried / it / cleaning / you / Have**) _____?

Greg: 4. (**but / Yes, / worse / made / it / I**) _____ .

Wes: 5. (**it / take / to / could / a / You / dry cleaner**) _____ .

Greg: That's a great idea, Wes! I'll do that now.

Language Focus

A **Complete the conversation.** Circle the correct answers.

Roy: Can I get some advice? I have an extra ticket to a soccer game. I know both my
          girlfriend and brother want to go. What 1. (**could / should**) I do?

Shelly: Well, have you tried 2. (**get / getting**) another ticket?

Roy: Yeah, but the game is already sold out.

Shelly: Why don't you 3. (**tell / telling**) both of them that there's just one ticket? Then you
          4. (**could / would**) let them decide who goes.

Roy: Ha! I don't think that will work.

Shelly: I know! You 5. (**should / would**) give one ticket to your brother and the other
          to your girlfriend.

Roy: But wait! Then I can't go.

B **Read the situations below.** Choose the better advice in each one.

IN CLASS Practice with a partner. Give reasons for your choice.

1. Terry: I have to give a speech in English, and I'm really nervous.

   Lina: I think you should (**practice more / be brave**).

2. Grace: I hate playing the flute, but my parents have already paid for all my lessons.

   Victor: Why don't you (**tell them you hate it / try it for a while**)?

3. Eddie: My friend wants to be a singer, but I think she's terrible at singing.

   Carol: If I were you, I'd (**say nothing / make fun of her**).

A **Skim the discussion thread.** Where is the best place for each of these sentences? Write the letters in the correct places. One is extra.

a. Everyone needs friends.   b. Now we're not talking.   c. It's not that easy to do!

Message Board

What's the worst advice you've ever gotten?   Submitted 2 weeks ago

Posted: 3:55 p.m. by **nkdexter**   Reply

I hate to say it, but it was from my father. He usually gives great advice, but last year I changed schools, and I didn't know anyone there. He said, "Don't bother making friends. Just study." I didn't take his advice. (1) _____

> **MauriceLePen**
>
> My father also gave me bad advice once. I love painting, and my dream has always been to be an artist. He suggested I quit being an artist and get a job as an art teacher. I did, and made more money, but I wasn't happy.

Posted: 3:59 p.m. by **KathyO'Connor75**   Reply

The worst advice? That's easy. A colleague told me I should buy a house right away. She said prices were going to go up soon. I bought a house, and prices started dropping the next month. It's now worth 60 percent of what I paid.

Posted: 4:05 p.m. by **sammylopez**   Reply

Sometimes I'm not happy about something, and it shows. My sister usually says something like, "You should smile more. It's a bad day, not a bad life."

> **celia123**
>
> I know what you mean. I get really nervous before exams. My teacher always says, "Just relax." (2) _____

B **Match the people to the descriptions.**

1. nkdexter ○   ○ a. gave up on his dream and was unhappy

2. MauriceLePen ○   ○ b. ignored a parent's advice

3. KathyO'Connor75 ○   ○ c. got advice from a sibling

4. sammylopez ○   ○ d. was told not to panic

5. celia123 ○   ○ e. made a bad investment

Reading

A **Skim the article.** Choose the best alternative title.

a. How to Give
   Advice

b. How to Ask
   for Advice

c. How to Take
   Advice

THE ART OF
ADVICE

For most people, asking for advice can be scary. In a study by Harvard Business School and the Wharton School of the University of Pennsylvania, 74 percent of 199 individuals said that they were afraid of asking for advice. But asking for advice is actually a good thing! People who ask for advice are more likely to succeed at a task, and get it done well. So how do you go about asking for advice? Here are a few tips.

Look for the best person to give you advice. It might be easy to ask all your social media contacts for advice at once, but will you value all advice equally? Probably not. It might be better to target one or two people whose opinions you value most. Ideally, you want to ask for advice from experts or people who have experience in the topic you're asking about. For example, if you want to lose weight, you could ask a fitness trainer at the local gym for advice on how to do it.

Give a clear context for your problem. For example, imagine you can't decide on the best way to organize a class presentation. When you ask for advice, you should mention the type of class, the topic, the audience, and the time allowed. It's also important to find the right time to ask. If what you are asking requires a lot of thought, approach the person when he or she is most clear headed. For some, this may mean in the morning, before they are overwhelmed with the tasks of the day. For others, it may mean at the end of the day, once they have cleared their to-do list. All of these things will help the person you are asking give better advice.

Be very specific in your questioning. Think of three to five questions that can be answered quickly. Imagine you want to own a business someday. Do you ask a business owner, "What advice do you have for me?" No, because it's not specific enough. It would be better to ask, "What college classes did you find helpful for starting a business?" or "I want to own a business someday. What skill sets should I be focusing on?"

Sometimes, you may need to ask for a second opinion. If you can't solve your problem by following your first advisor's advice, ask someone else who may have a different perspective on the issue. The key is: The next time you need advice, don't be afraid to ask.

B Check (✓) the sentences the author would probably agree with.

1. _____ Ask as many people as you can for advice.

2. _____ Choose the right time to ask.

3. _____ Have a list of specific questions.

4. _____ Give detailed background information.

5. _____ Ask for a second opinion.

6. _____ Ask only questions that can be answered by *Yes* or *No*.

C Read the article. Number the tips given in order (**1–5**). One is extra.

_____ Get a second opinion.   _____ Be specific.   _____ Return the favor.

_____ Give a clear context.   _____ Ask the right person.   _____ Ask at the right time.

Writing

WRITING TIP Adding support to your writing

You can make your writing clearer and easier to read by adding support such as **examples**, **facts**, **anecdotes**, or **quotes**.

For example, **if you want to lose weight, you could ask a fitness trainer at the local gym for advice on how to do it.** (an example)

In a study by Harvard Business School and the Wharton School of the University of Pennsylvania, **74 percent of 199 individuals said that they were afraid of asking for advice.** (a fact)

Each child learns differently. **My father used to use board games to teach me vocabulary and mathematics.** **Make learning interesting for children.** (an anecdote)

Don't be afraid of doing things differently. **As Steve Jobs said, "Innovation distinguishes between a leader and a follower."** (a quote)

A **Think of a problem you would like advice on.** On a separate piece of paper, write an email asking someone for advice. Include examples, facts, anecdotes, or quotes to add support to your writing. Use the outline method you learned in Unit 1.

B **IN CLASS** Share your emails.

THE KOALA WAS TAKEN TO A SHELTER.

Vocabulary Focus

A Match. Join the words to the definitions.

1. abandon ○   ○ a. to collect something or someone
2. calm down ○   ○ b. to leave and not return
3. pick up ○   ○ c. to clean (usually with soap and water)
4. place ○   ○ d. to make someone or something feel relaxed
5. remove ○   ○ e. to take away
6. wash ○   ○ f. to put

B Complete the sentences. Use the words in the box.

> adopt   attached   decorate   release   treated   wrapped

1. When the turtles get big enough, we can _____ them back into the water.

2. After the vet _____ the sick bird for a few days, it was well enough to fly.

3. You could _____ your office with a plant or some pictures.

4. The animal rescue officer _____ the baby bird in a towel to calm it down.

5. My sister wants to _____ a dog from the animal shelter.

6. The scientists _____ a tag to the koala's ear so they could monitor it.

Conversation

Complete the conversation. Put the sentences in the correct order.
IN CLASS Practice with a partner.

a. _____ No, it was taken to a vet.

b. _____ The poor thing. Did someone take it to an animal shelter?

c. _____ I don't think so. I think it was just scared.

d. _____ Why? Was it hurt?

e. __1__ Did you hear? A baby fox was found behind the school yesterday!

f. _____ Then it's probably all right to take it to a shelter. When it's older, it can be released back into the wild.

Language Focus

A **Complete the story.** Use the correct forms of the words in parentheses.

It was a cold, dark night. A small squirrel with a broken leg (1) _____ (**find**) outside the animal shelter just before closing time. It was dirty and looked cold, so it (2) _____ (**give**) a warm bath by Layla, the shelter vet. It then (3) _____ (**wrap**) in a blanket. It didn't move, even when Layla (4) _____ (**hold**) it, so she (5) _____ (**decide**) to give it some food. "Poor baby. You look hungry!" she (6) _____ (**say**) as she went to get some food. When she got back to the room, she was surprised. The squirrel wasn't there! Where was it? She couldn't find it. Layla (7) _____ (**run**) outside and . . .

B **Read the sentences.** Then rewrite them.

1. They took the dog to the animal shelter. _The dog was taken to the animal shelter_ .

2. Someone saw two large bears near the lake. _____ .

3. Someone has released the koala into the wild. _____ .

4. Someone checked and treated the injured owl. _____ .

5. They tagged the injured animals. _____ .

C **Read the story in A again.** What do you think happened next? Write the next part of the story.
IN CLASS Discuss with a partner.

The Real World

A **Skim the article below.** How was the Photo Ark successful?

a. It allowed a species to breed in captivity.

b. It helped raise awareness of a species' decline.

c. It allowed a species to be removed from the endangered species list.

Home   **BLOG**   Photos   Contact   About Me

Photo Ark Success Story
By Joel Sartore

It was almost too late when I first learned of the Florida grasshopper sparrow's troubles. Down to just a few hundred, the bird was in sudden decline. Biologists were unclear why.

In 2012, writer Ted Williams, biologist Paul Miller, and I traveled to Kissimmee Prairie Preserve State Park in Florida, U.S.A. We found a singing male grasshopper sparrow running about defending his mating territory. Paul caught the bird, and I put it in my little photo box. And with that, the Florida grasshopper sparrow was on board the Photo Ark.

A year later, *Audubon* magazine put the bird on its cover with the words, "End of the Line?" Between that and social media, people started to take notice of this tiny bird. The U.S. Fish and Wildlife Service has provided over a million dollars to help fight the bird's extinction. Intensive study and perhaps even captive breeding can now begin.

The Photo Ark has done its job.

B **Match.** Join the people and organizations to the actions.

1. Paul Miller	a. gave money to protect the bird
2. Joel Sartore	b. published a photograph of the bird
3. *Audubon* magazine	c. photographed the bird
4. U.S. Fish and Wildlife Service	d. caught the bird

Reading

A **Scan the article.** Write the names of the countries mentioned in the article on the map below.

SAVING **DUNIA**

She may look like any other baby gorilla, but Dunia is special. When she was still a baby, some hunters wanted to sell her as a pet. She was caught in Africa, in the Democratic Republic of the Congo. Then, she was put in a sports bag and taken east to nearby Rwanda to a man who said that he would buy her. Luckily, this man was actually working with the police, and he drove Dunia to the Mountain Gorilla Veterinary Project, a group of people that take care of the area's 700 or so wild mountain gorillas.

When the people at the Mountain Gorilla Veterinary Project saw Dunia, they knew she wasn't well. She needed water and food, so she was given green beans, pineapple, bananas, and milk. Even more than food, the project members knew she needed love and comfort. Gorillas are known for being big and strong, but what many people don't know is that baby gorillas need physical contact with their mothers to be healthy. According to the project vet, Chris Whittier, baby gorillas can't survive if they aren't held by their mothers. The project members knew this, so they gave Dunia around-the-clock care and took turns holding her. It wasn't easy at first. Dunia tried to get away and resisted attention. "Dunia needed contact, but there was no reason that she should trust people after what she'd been through," Whittier says. "Humans had killed her family."

After six months of loving care, Dunia was finally looking and acting like a happy, healthy young gorilla. "Her confidence is growing, and she's becoming more independent," says Whittier. However, when she gets scared, she still runs back to the people who are caring for her, just like she would to her mother. Over time, Dunia started to go out farther and for longer periods of time. In 2011, vets at the project were able to return Dunia to the Democratic Republic of the Congo and release her into a gorilla sanctuary.

B **Complete the summary.** Use words from the article.

Some hunters wanted to make some money. They wanted to sell Dunia as a (1) _____ . A man in Rwanda said he would (2) _____ her. He took her to the Mountain Gorilla Veterinary Project. When Dunia arrived there, she needed (3) _____ and (4) _____ . She was given lots of fruits and vegetables. But baby gorillas that aren't held by their mothers can't (5) _____ .

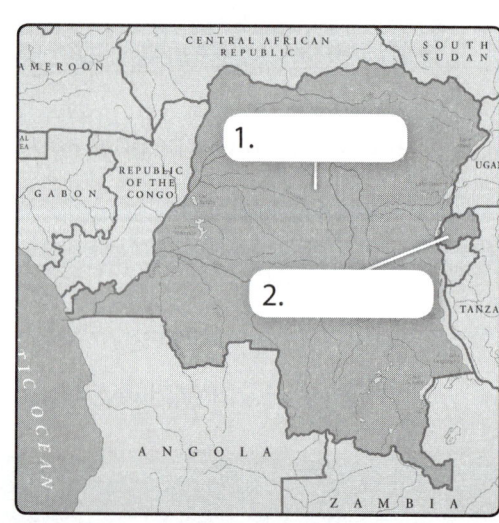

The project members took turns (6) _____ her. Soon, Dunia began looking and acting like a happy and (7) _____ young gorilla. Eventually, the project members were able to release her into a gorilla sanctuary.

Writing

WRITING TIP **Using sensory details in a story**

When you describe an event or tell a story, use sensory details to help "paint a picture" for the reader. These kinds of details show how they affect our five senses.

Sight: light blue water, big round eyes, a child smiling _____

Smell: salty air, fresh bread, burning meat _____

Hearing: a loud cry, a buzzing sound, shouting for joy _____

Taste: sweet milk, strong tea, sour fruit _____

Touch: cool water, hot sun, a hand on my shoulder _____

A **Add one more example for each sense.**

B **Read the beginning and end of the story below.** Write the middle. Include some sensory details to make the story more interesting.

Manatee Rescue!

Richard Dash stood there in the hot sun watching the scared baby manatee in the river. She was alone and crying pitifully for her mother. But her mother was not there. She might have been scared away by the loud roar of a passing motorboat. Even with a net, Dash knew he could not catch the manatee. He called rescue workers for help.

After the manatee was safe in the pool, the rescue team rushed her to a zoo. The baby needed many months of care. She was introduced to a female manatee. This female acted as the baby's mother. After five months together, the baby and her "new" mother were released into a river nearby. The rescue team clapped as the mother and baby swam away.

C **IN CLASS** **Share your stories.** Take turns reading them.

1.

2.

HOW WAS IT FORMED?

Vocabulary Focus

A **Label the photos.** Use the words in the box.

> arch   cave   glacier   tower   valley

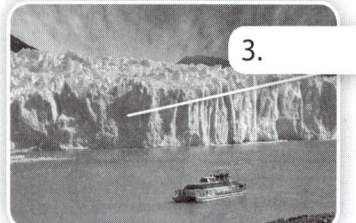
3.

4.

5.

B **Complete the sentences.** Use the phrases in the box.

> agree on   look after   pay for   pull over   put out   wear down

1. The firefighters were able to _____ the fire very quickly.

2. Wind and water have started to _____ the face of this rock.

3. I'd like to buy this book. Where do I _____ it?

4. My grandparents _____ me when my parents are away.

5. I feel a little carsick. Could you _____ for a while?

6. We need to _____ where we want to go: Devil's Tower or Death Valley.

Conversation

Complete the interview. Circle the correct answers.
IN CLASS Practice with a partner.

Host: Welcome! Our guest today is geologist Dr. Herbert Lee. So, Dr. Lee, you've brought some photos of very interesting landscapes. Can you tell us how these landscapes were 1. (**formed** / **worn**)?

Dr. Lee: Well, the places you see in these photos have been 2. (**created** / **eaten**) away and 3. (**worn** / **formed**) down by wind and water. Some of these rocks have also been 4. (**eaten** / **broken**) apart by ice.

Host: Wow, this is a great photo! Where is this?

Dr. Lee: This is Krabi, in southern Thailand. Those are limestone mountains. However, as the number of tourists increases, some of these caves have been 5. (**damaged** / **broken**) by the carbon dioxide produced when people breathe.

Host: I bet there are many more interesting things you can tell us, Dr. Lee. Keep watching. We'll be back after this short break.

Language Focus

A **Complete the information.** Circle the correct answers.

The Eye of the Sahara

The Eye of the Sahara is a colorful rock structure in Mauritania, in western Africa. When it 1. (**views** / **is viewed**) from above, the circular, dome-like structure 2. (**looks** / **is looked**) like a giant bull's-eye. People once 3. (**thought** / **is thought**) that it 4. (**created** / **was created**) by a meteor that struck the Earth many years ago. However, it was in fact formed from uplifted rock. This rock 5. (**eroded** / **was eroded**) by wind over many years. The structure is 40 kilometers wide and can 6. (**see** / **be seen**) by astronauts from space.

B **Read the sentences.** Then rewrite them in the passive form.

1. Wind has eaten away at this rock. This rock has been eaten away by wind   .

2. Ocean waves are wearing away the rock. _____ .

3. Freezing water forms tiny cracks in rocks. _____ .

4. A meteor created the Vredefort crater. _____ .

5. Heavy rain has eroded the soil. _____ .

The Real World

A **Skim the article.** Write the letters of the subheadings in the correct places.

a. What to do   b. How to get there   c. What to buy   d. Where to stay

Aogashima

Imagine a picture-perfect volcanic island in the Pacific. But this island is unusual. On Aogashima, people actually live inside a volcano! The island's town of 170 people has a single school, a general store, and a post office. Life on the island is peaceful.

1. _____ Aogashima, which means "blue island," lies 368 kilometers south of Tokyo, Japan. It's not an easy place to get to. Travelers take a ferry from Tokyo to Hachijo Island. From there, they have a choice of another ferry or a helicopter.

2. _____ There are several *minshukus*, or Japanese inns, in the town. All of them provide meals with your stay—there are no restaurants on the island. Another option is camping, which is free.

3. _____ Scuba diving is popular, as are hiking and visiting hot springs. The main volcano has scalding hot steam vents around one side, which are used to power the public sauna. You can even cook food at these steam vents—in pots left outside the sauna.

4. _____ Visitors don't come to Aogashima for the shopping, but if you're looking to take something home, consider salt. It's made by drying seawater over the volcanic vents.

If you are planning a trip, remember that Aogashima is an active volcano. The last eruption was in 1785—over 200 years ago. About 140 people died then. So be sure to keep an eye on the volcanic conditions.

B **Read the article.** Circle the correct answers.

1. This article is meant for _____ Aogashima.

    a. visitors to   b. residents of   c. students of

2. There is no _____ route connecting Aogashima and Hachijo.

    a. air   b. land   c. sea

3. What must you do if you want to camp on Aogashima?

    a. bring food   b. find a *minshuku*   c. pay for your campsite in advance

Reading

A **Read the encyclopedia entry below.** Check (✓) the questions that are answered in the article.

1. _____ What is a fjord?

2. _____ Where is the world's deepest fjord?

3. _____ What are cold-water organisms?

4. _____ Where is the world's longest fjord?

5. _____ How are fjords formed?

6. _____ What is a skerry?

Encyclopedia Entry | Fjords

fjord /fyôrd/ (also **fiord**)

A fjord is a long, deep, narrow body of water that reaches far inland. Fjords are often set in a U-shaped valley with steep walls of rock on three sides. Fjords are found mainly in Norway, Chile, New Zealand, Canada, Greenland, and the U.S. state of Alaska. At 350 kilometers long, Scoresby Sund in Greenland is the longest fjord in the world.

Fjords were created by glaciers. During the Earth's last ice age, glaciers covered just about everything. Glaciers move very slowly, and can greatly change the landscape they move through. Deep valleys are formed through this process. When a glacier retreats, seawater fills in the empty space it leaves. This is why fjords can be thousands of meters deep. Fjords are usually deepest farther inland, where the glacial force was the strongest. This is because rock is left at the mouth of the fjord when the glacier retreats.

Skerries are small, rocky islands created through glaciation. They are found both in and around fjords. Much of the coastline of Norway is cut into thousands of skerries. The U.S. states of Washington and Alaska also have skerries. Even though skerries can be hard to get around in a boat, fjords have generally calm waters. This makes them popular harbors for ships. Fjords are also becoming more and more popular as cruise ship destinations.

A number of fjords include coral reefs. Some very large coral reefs are found at the bottom of fjords in Norway. They are home to several types of fish, plankton, and other sea creatures. Some coral reefs are also found in the fjords of New Zealand. Scientists know much less about these deep, cold-water reefs than they do about tropical coral reefs. But they have learned that the living things in cold-water reefs prefer total darkness. Organisms in cold-water reefs have also adapted to life under very high pressure. At the bottom of a fjord, the water pressure can be hundreds or even thousands of kilograms per square meter. Few organisms can survive in this cold, dark habitat.

B **Complete the summary.** Use words from the article.

(1) _____ were formed by glaciers. When a glacier retreats, the empty space is filled with (2) _____. The deepest part of a fjord is usually farther (3) _____. The mouth of the fjord is shallower because (4) _____ is left behind when the glacier retreats. (5) _____ are small, rocky islands. They can be found in and around fjords, making it difficult to get around in boats. However, the calm waters of fjords make them great harbors for ships, or as (6) _____ ship destinations. Fjords are also home to many sea creatures. These creatures prefer living in total (7) _____ and under very high (8) _____.

C **IN CLASS** **Talk with a partner.** Describe an interesting land formation that you've visited.

Writing

WRITING TIP **Informal and formal writing**

When you write, think about what type of text you are writing and who is going to read it. This will tell you how formal your writing should be.

INFORMAL WRITING	FORMAL WRITING
Emails, texts, memos, chats	Articles, essays, business letters
Frequent abbreviations or contractions	No abbreviations or contractions
Use of slang, phrasal verbs, and idioms	No slang, phrasal verbs, and idioms
More use of active voice	More use of passive voice

A **Classify these sentences.** Write **I** for Informal or **F** for Formal.

1. _____ Let's meet at 5:30 at the library to hang out. See you then!

2. _____ The hikers were not rescued until six o'clock the next day.

3. _____ I'm a bit under the weather. I think I'll just rest at home.

4. _____ The man was stopped by the police. He was then asked to show his license.

B **Write a newspaper article.** Imagine you write for a school newspaper. Write a report about a recent natural disaster. What caused it? What happened?

C **IN CLASS** Share your articles.

6

LOOK AT THAT NARWHAL!

Vocabulary Focus

A **Match.** Read the descriptions. Then write the names of the animals.

> whale shark   otter   narwhal   jellyfish

1. I live in the Arctic Ocean. I have a tusk, which is very long. I am known as the unicorn of the sea. What am I? _____

2. I live in many of the world's oceans and seas. I have a soft body, and I use my mouth to move. Some people like to eat me. What am I? _____

3. I am the largest fish in the ocean, but I am a very gentle animal. My body is blue with white dots. I eat plankton, krill, and very small fish. What am I? _____

4. I live mostly in freshwater rivers. My cousin lives in the Pacific Ocean. I'm covered in fur and sometimes float on my back. I look a little like a seal. What am I? _____

B **Complete the chart.** Check (✓) the things these animals have.

	FEATHERS	FLIPPERS	FINS	A SHELL	A TAIL
penguin					
crab					
flying fish					
dugong					
turtle					
dolphin					
albatross					

Conversation

Look at the picture. Circle the correct words to complete the conversation.

IN CLASS Practice with a partner.

Katya: Hi, Ravi. Great picture! Where was it taken?

Ravi: At the aquarium. I went there yesterday with my cousins. That's Carlos on the left. That toy 1. (**otter** / **hermit crab**), 2. (**which** / **who**) he bought at the gift shop, is ten times bigger than a real one.

Katya: It's so cute! Who's next to Carlos—the boy 3. (**who's** / **which is**) wearing a baseball cap?

Ravi: That's his brother, Marc. That 4. (**dugong** / **shark**) T-shirt he's wearing only cost $5.

Katya: Cool! How about the girl on the right 5. (**which is** / **who's**) holding the turtle?

Ravi: That's Ana. She's the oldest.

Language Focus

A **Combine the sentences using *which* or *who*.**

1. The Great Barrier Reef is popular with divers. It is home to many marine species.

   _____

2. Clownfish live in small groups. They are usually orange and white.

   _____

3. My brother works at an aquarium. He studied marine biology in college.

   _____

4. Sally is a volunteer at the zoo. She's very interested in animals.

   _____

B **Write sentences about Antarctica.** Use the information given.

1. Antarctica / always covered in ice and snow / coldest continent on Earth

   _____

2. The emperor penguin / largest penguin in the world / lives only in Antarctica

   _____

3. The leopard seal / got its name from the way it looks / one of the main predators in Antarctica

   _____

The Real World

A **Skim the article.** Choose the best title.

a. The Beauty of Sharks   b. Design by Nature   c. Why Sharks Have Scales

Sharks are best known for their teeth. But recently, their scales have been getting a lot of attention. Shark scales have provided an inspiration for design.

When viewed under a microscope, the skin of a shark is made up of countless tiny scales. These scales have lines that run down the length of its body. This allows the shark to swim through water smoothly and quickly.

Scientists soon picked up on this idea. One swimsuit manufacturer has created material that uses a similar design. A swimsuit made of this fabric received a lot of attention during the 2004 Olympics, when swimmer Michael Phelps wore a sharkskin swimsuit. Many people said the suit gave him the winning edge. By 2008, nearly every Olympic medal winner wore a sharkskin swimsuit.

Swimsuit designers have since created full-body suits that cover the arms and legs. The suits are very expensive, and many say they offer swimmers an unfair advantage. In 2010, the International Swimming Federation voted to ban the use of these high-tech suits.

B **Read the article.** Circle **T** for True or **F** for False.

1. A shark's scales help it to swim fast.   T   F

2. Scientists created swimsuits from real shark scales.   T   F

3. Some people are unhappy because they feel the use of   T   F
   sharkskin swimsuits is unfair to others.

4. The word "ban" can be replaced with the word "support."   T   F

Reading

A **Skim the article.** What is the main idea of the article?

   a. Artificial reefs are attracting tourists.

   b. Subway cars are polluting the ocean.

   c. Subway cars are being used to create artificial reefs.

SUBWAY **SHELTER**

Along the Atlantic coast of the United States, thousands of fish are crowded into subway cars, but they're going nowhere, and fishermen couldn't be happier. The subway cars were placed in the ocean to serve as artificial reefs.

When New York City transportation officials wanted to recycle more than a thousand subway cars in 2001, the artificial reef program seemed like an ideal solution. Before the rail cars were sunk, all dangerous materials were removed. The doors and windows were taken off and the interiors were cleaned. What remained were 9,000-kilogram boxes with good water circulation and lots of areas for fish to hide in. The cars were then dropped from ships, and they sank to the ocean floor. Over 1,200 cars were dropped into the ocean.

Hard surfaces—whether natural or human-made—are attractive to oysters, mussels, and other food sources important to local fish populations. But most of the ocean floor along the mid-Atlantic is bare sand. "In the mid-Atlantic region, we have very, very little exposed rock," said Jeff Tinsman, who coordinated the placement of the subway cars. These artificial reefs therefore quickly attract marine life. Divers to the reefs often report seeing hundreds of black sea bass—an important fish for the local economy.

Each year, fish and wildlife agencies in the region release guides for the artificial reefs. Fishermen use these to find the best fishing spots. Local agencies manage reef fish populations the same way they do any other fishery, setting limits on the size and number of fish that can be caught.

Michael Zacchea oversees the recycling of subway cars for the New York City Transit Authority. Since 2007, the agency has recycled at least 2,500 more subway cars. Zacchea said using the cars for reefs "was more successful than we ever considered it would be. It was a great program all around."

B **Complete the summary.** Use words from the article.

On the Atlantic coast of the United States, thousands of (1) _____ cars from
New York City have been dropped into the (2) _____ to create artificial reefs.
Each 9,000-kilogram car is first stripped bare of all doors, windows, and any other
(3) _____ materials. The interiors are then (4) _____ thoroughly. In the
mid-Atlantic region, there is little exposed (5) _____, so the cars act as a
(6) _____ surface to attract marine life. Local agencies manage the reef fish
population, setting limits on the size and (7) _____ of fish that can be caught.
The artificial reef program has been very (8) _____.

Writing

WRITING TIP **Adding variety with synonyms**

To make your writing more interesting, use synonyms so you don't repeat the same word
many times. Notice the synonyms in these sentences.

**The injured animal was able to quickly escape the hunter. Although it was hurt, it
was still able to run fast.**

**The little fish needed to find a place to hide before the shark found it. After it found the
perfect spot in the coral reef, the tiny creature did not move until the shark swam away.**

A **Read the notice below.** Find a synonym in the paragraph for each bold word.

talk   _____   big   _____   struck   _____

spilled   _____   occurred   _____

You Can Help

Animals can't **talk**, but if they could speak to us, they would probably ask us to help
protect them from oil spills. Oil spills happen when **big** ships that carry oil—called
tankers—become damaged and leak oil into the ocean. On March 24, 1989, one of
these huge tankers, called the *Exxon Valdez*, **struck** Bligh Reef in Alaska. After it hit
the reef, an enormous amount of oil **spilled** into the ocean. More recently, on April
20, 2010, another oil spill **occurred** in the Gulf of Mexico. Oil leaked into the water for
nearly three months. These are just two of the biggest oil spills that have ever
happened! Oil spills like these hurt all kinds of animals.

B **Research a cause that is important to you.** Then write a paragraph explaining what
your cause is and what you can do to help.

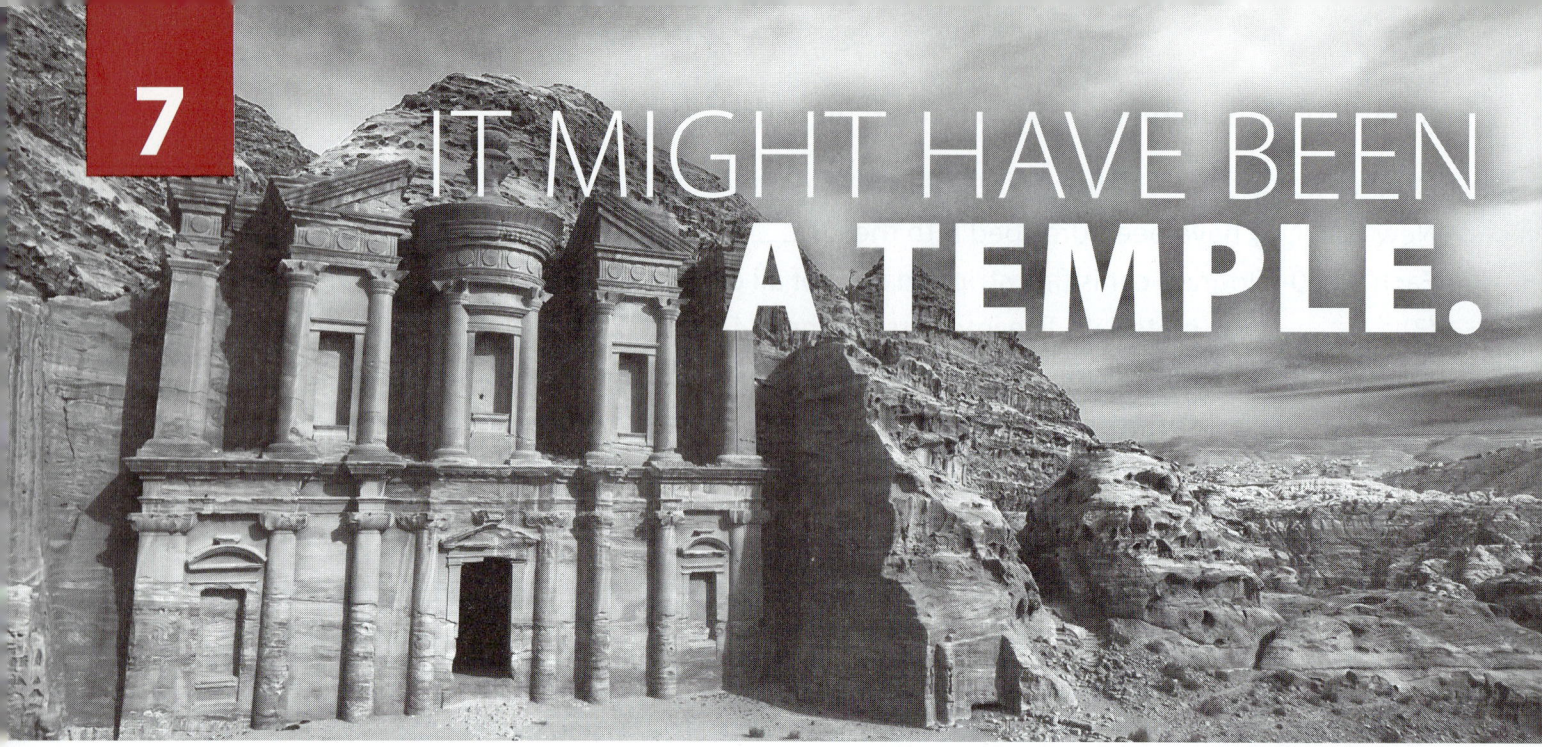

7 IT MIGHT HAVE BEEN A TEMPLE.

Vocabulary Focus

A **Complete the sentences.** Use the words in the box.

gold	temples	statue	jewelry	treasure
farming	diseases	religion	invaded	civilization

1. The bride wore gold _____ worth over $30,000.

2. The ruins of ancient _____ in Cambodia show that _____ played an important role in ancient civilizations.

3. Archaeologists discovered a three-meter-tall _____ in the Mediterranean Sea.

4. Irrigation and _____ allowed the early Indus Valley _____ to thrive.

5. The _____ that they dug up contained mostly silver and _____ coins.

6. After the Spanish _____ Peru, they introduced _____ that killed many Inca.

B **Circle the word that is different.**

1. farming   jewelry   treasure

2. invader   temple   religion

3. farming   gold   irrigation

4. artifact   archaeologist   disease

Conversation

Complete the conversation. Circle the correct answers.

IN CLASS Practice with a partner.

Todd: Look at this coin I got on my trip to Italy!

Tanya: Wow! Do you know who the man on the coin is?

Todd: Yes! It 1. (**can't** / **must**) be Julius Caesar. See—the image looks just like him. And his name is here in Latin. You know, Cleopatra lived at the same time as Caesar. She 2. (**could** / **must**) have held this very coin!

Tanya: Cool! That's possible. Is the coin made of gold?

Todd: Yeah, it 3. (**could** / **can't**) be gold. Caesar produced the greatest number of gold coins in Rome. Or it 4. (**might** / **must**) be bronze, but I'm not sure.

Tanya: So where did you find this coin?

Todd: Oh, I didn't find it. I bought it from a guy on the street—for three euros.

Tanya: Oh, no! I think he 5. (**may** / **should**) have cheated you. A real Roman coin is worth much more than that.

Language Focus

A **Complete the sentences.** Use the correct forms of the words in parentheses.

1. Tutankhamun _____ (**might, die**) from a war injury.

2. Their weapons _____ (**can't, be**) made of metal. People were still using stone at that time.

3. The river _____ (**could, dry up**) because of a drought in the region.

4. The treasure _____ (**might, not be**) here anymore. Robbers might have stolen it.

B **Match.** Join the observations to the guesses.

1. There's a laptop on the desk.   ○   ○ a. It might be for a party.

2. The ground is wet.   ○   ○ b. It must have been taken a long time ago.

3. The picture has turned yellow.   ○   ○ c. It could be Lisa's. She was studying just now.

4. There's a nice big meal on the table.   ○   ○ d. It must have rained earlier.

The Real World

A Scan the article. Write the dates.

1. Fortress found: _____

2. Carbon dating done: _____

3. Fortress built: _____

Lost to History

A team of archaeologists has confirmed that a fortress in southwest Mongolia was built by the Mongol leader Genghis Khan. The fortress, which was discovered in 2001, measures 170 meters by 200 meters, and has thick walls made out of hard soil. Archaeologists uncovered animal bones, wood fragments, and Chinese ceramics at the site.

In 2014, archaeologists used carbon dating to date these artifacts to between the 12th and 14th centuries. They concluded that the fortress must have been a military base during Genghis Khan's invasion of Central Asia. They believe that the base was probably built in 1212 and was used as the Khan expanded his army westward. After the decline of the Mongol Empire in the 14th century, the fortress fell into ruin. It eventually became lost to history.

Koichi Matsuda, professor of Mongol Empire history at Osaka International University, was the expedition's team leader. He hopes the discovery will help explain the history of this region of Mongolia between the 13th and 14th centuries.

B Read the article. Circle the correct answers.

1. Another title for this reading could be _____.

   a. The Death of Khan   b. The Mongol Empire   c. An Ancient Fortress

2. What is a fortress?

   a. a military base   b. a buried tomb   c. a place to store ceramics

3. The fortress probably fell into ruin because the Mongols _____ it.

   a. destroyed   b. stopped using   c. buried

Reading

A **Skim the article.** Circle **T** for True or **F** for False.

1. A mummy is a living being.   T   F

2. The mummy in the tomb was a young woman.   T   F

3. This mummy was unusual because women were   T   F
   not considered to be important in ancient Peru.

THE MYSTERY OF
THE MUMMY

Inside an ancient building in Peru, archaeologists found a tomb. The tomb was built by the Moche, a civilization that controlled northern Peru from A.D. 100 to A.D. 800.

After digging carefully for several weeks, the team of archaeologists found one of the world's best-preserved mummies. They were surprised to find gold nose rings, necklaces, and weapons that were usually only used by the best soldiers. Based on this, the team assumed that the mummy must have been a powerful person, and probably a man. However, when the gold bowl that was covering the mummy's face was removed, they discovered that the mummy wasn't a man at all. It was actually a young woman who was probably in her 20s when she died.

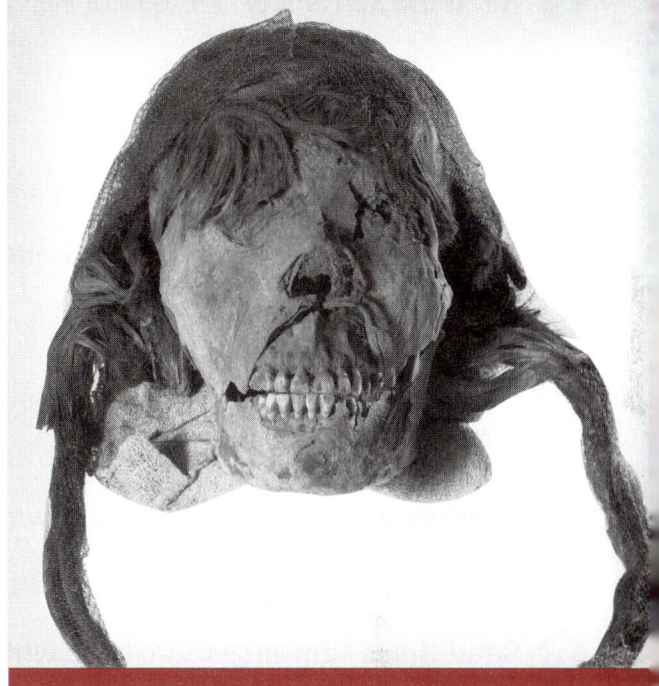

Lots of Questions

The archaeologists were excited, but now they had even more questions. This was an unusual mummy—the first discovery of its kind. Sixteen centuries ago in Peru, women were not considered very important in society. So who was she? She was put in the tomb with all these treasures, so she couldn't have been a regular person. She was also unusual because she had tattoos—drawings on the skin of her arms, legs, and feet—of animals like snakes, spiders, and crabs. The experts couldn't understand what these tattoos meant or why she was buried this way.

No Answers

The archaeologists have studied the mummy and the area where they found her, but they still haven't been able to answer most of their questions. For example, she didn't seem to be hurt or sick, so why did she die when she was so young? They don't know yet, but they do know that whoever she was, she must have been very important in her time.

B **Read the article.** Put the events in the order they occurred (**1–6**).

a. _____ The woman died.

b. _____ The archaeologists learned that the woman was not sick when she died.

c. _____ The Moche civilization started controlling northern Peru.

d. _____ The archaeologists found the mummy's tomb.

e. _____ A gold bowl was put over the woman's face.

f. _____ The tomb was sealed shut.

C **Read the sentences.** Write **F** for Fact or **O** for Opinion.

1. _____ The mummy could have been a soldier.

2. _____ A long time ago, women were not usually put in tombs with many treasures.

3. _____ The tattoos on the mummy's arms, legs, and feet are beautiful.

4. _____ The cause of the woman's death is still unknown.

Writing

WRITING TIP **Developing paragraphs by giving reasons**

When giving your opinion in a piece of writing, it's important to give reasons to support it.

A **Read these sentences.** Circle the writer's opinion in each sentence. Underline the reason the writer gives to support his or her opinion.

The mummy must have been an important person since her tomb contained a lot of treasure.

These ruins are important because they show that religion is older than civilization.

The tomb contained several weapons, so it might have been the tomb of a warrior.

B **Read the article about the mummy on page 37 again.** Write three ideas about who you think she might have been.

The woman could have been the queen.

C **Write a paragraph.** Choose one of your opinions in **B**. Write a paragraph giving reasons to explain your opinion.

IN CLASS Share your paragraphs.

8 IT'S TALLER THAN THE EIFFEL TOWER!

Vocabulary Focus

A **Find the hidden word.** Use the given clues to solve the puzzle.

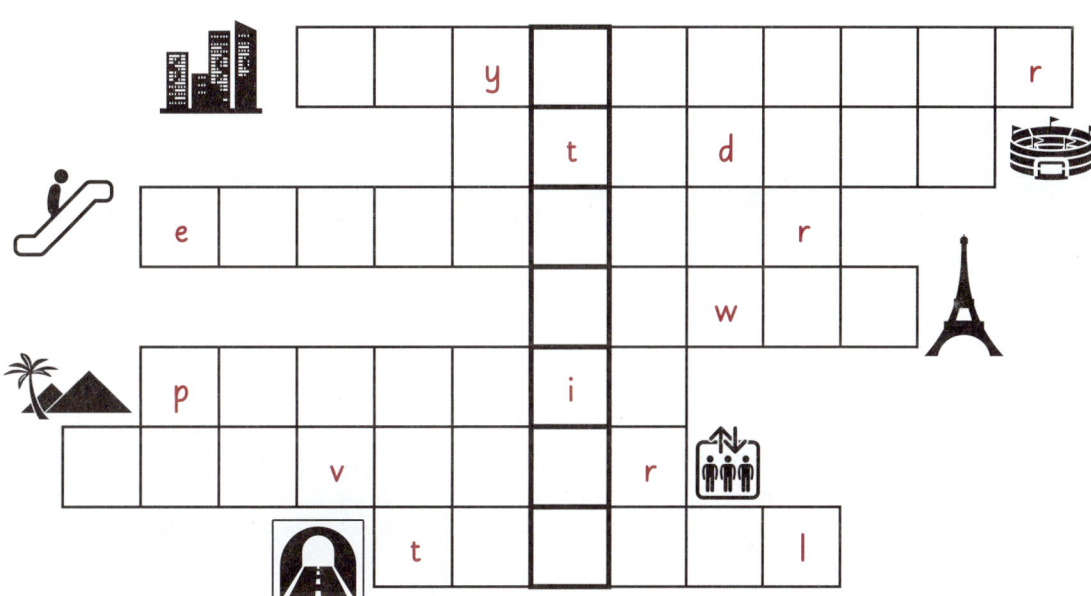

The hidden word is _____.

B **Complete the sentences.** Use the correct forms of the words in parentheses.

1. The Shanghai Transrapid is the _____ (**fast**) train in the world.

2. Tokyo city is _____ (**big**) than Bangkok.

3. The Y-40 Deep Joy is the _____ (**deep**) swimming pool in the world.

4. I think Angel Falls is _____ (**beautiful**) than Niagara Falls.

5. The view from this tower is _____ (**not, good**) the view from that skyscraper.

Conversation

Read the conversation and correct five mistakes.

IN CLASS Practice with a partner.

Rosa: How was Mexico City, Jack?

Jack: It was goodest vacation I've had! I spent most of my time at the Zócalo. I think it's the larger public square in the world.

Rosa: How was the food? Did you try any street food?

Jack: I ate street food all the time. It's not as expensive than the food in the restaurants. And I think it was tastiest.

Rosa: Did you get outside the city?

Jack: I did. I climbed up the Pyramid of the Sun.

Rosa: How fun! I wish I was enough fit to climb things like pyramids!

Language Focus

A **Complete the blog post.** Use the correct forms of the words in parentheses.

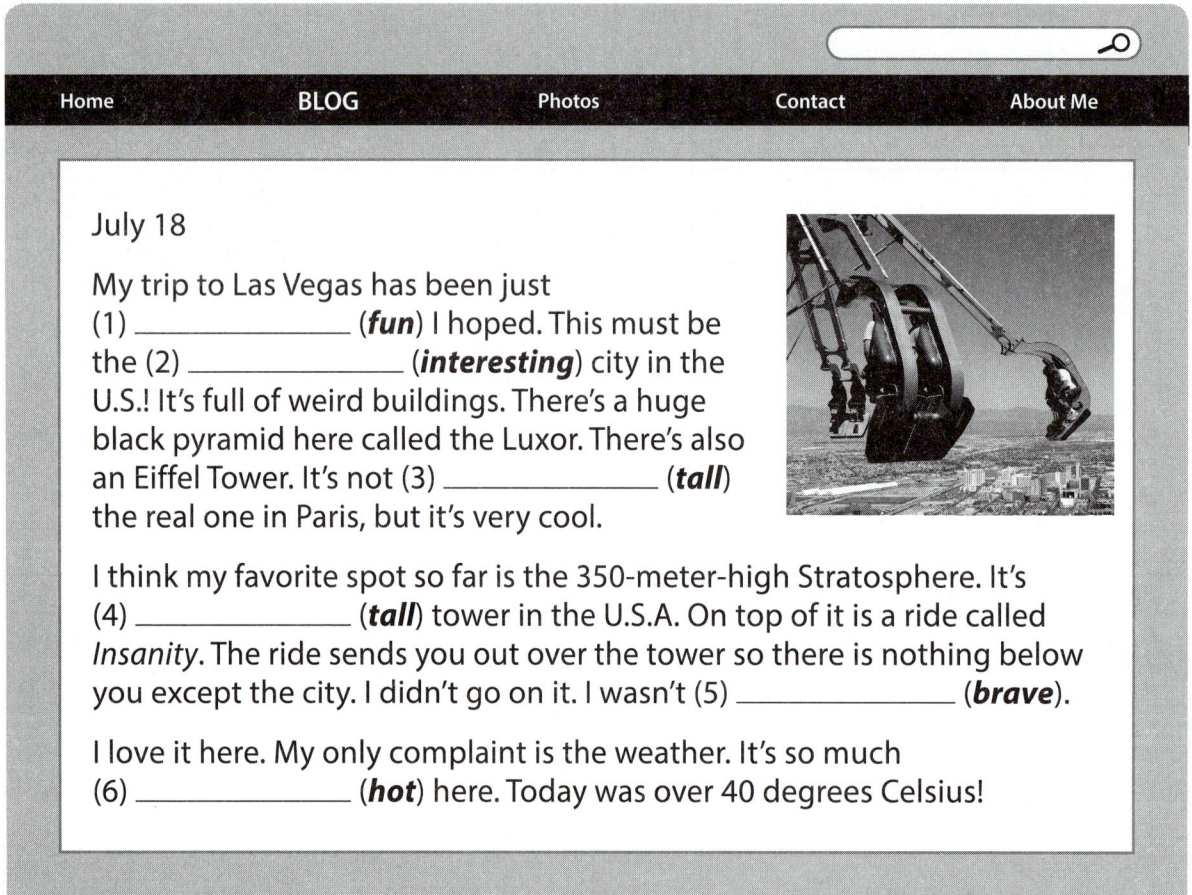

Home | BLOG | Photos | Contact | About Me

July 18

My trip to Las Vegas has been just (1) _____ (**fun**) I hoped. This must be the (2) _____ (**interesting**) city in the U.S.! It's full of weird buildings. There's a huge black pyramid here called the Luxor. There's also an Eiffel Tower. It's not (3) _____ (**tall**) the real one in Paris, but it's very cool.

I think my favorite spot so far is the 350-meter-high Stratosphere. It's (4) _____ (**tall**) tower in the U.S.A. On top of it is a ride called *Insanity*. The ride sends you out over the tower so there is nothing below you except the city. I didn't go on it. I wasn't (5) _____ (**brave**).

I love it here. My only complaint is the weather. It's so much (6) _____ (**hot**) here. Today was over 40 degrees Celsius!

B **Complete the sentences.** Circle the correct answers.

1. The clock tower is (**tall** / **taller**) than the school. It's also (**newer** / **newest**).

2. The (**quicker** / **quickest**) way to travel from Singapore to Thailand is by plane.

3. I love to travel. My (**most** / **more**) memorable trip was to Brazil.

4. The train tickets were (**cheaper** / **more cheap**) than the bus tickets. I never expected that!

The Real World

The Deep Joy

Are you the type of person who immediately heads for the deep end of your local swimming pool? If so, you'd love the pool at the Hotel Millepini Terme in the small town of Montegrotto Terme, Italy.

The Y-40, or "The Deep Joy" pool, reaches a depth of 40 meters, making it the deepest swimming pool in the world. That's equal to the height of a 14-story building. The pool holds 4.3 million liters of warm water from the nearby hot springs. The pool was designed for recreational scuba diving, scuba dive training, and free diving—deep diving without the use of scuba equipment.

The pool attracts divers from around the world. There is a special tunnel inside the pool for people who want to see the divers, but who don't want to get wet. The designers of the pool hope it will help transform the small town into a world-class diving center.

A **Match.** Find synonyms for the words below in the article.

1. goes toward: _____   2. the same as: _____   3. tools: _____

4. brings in: _____   5. change: _____   6. first-rate: _____

B **Read the article.** Circle **T** for True or **F** for False.

1. The deepest swimming pool in the world is located in Italy.   **T**   **F**

2. The pool was designed for scientists to study deep-sea creatures.   **T**   **F**

3. The water for the pool comes from nearby hot springs.   **T**   **F**

4. The designers of the pool hope it will draw more tourists to   **T**   **F**
   Montegrotto Terme.

Reading

A **Skim the article.** Which situation does the diagram show?

a. the SMART tunnel during regular use

b. the SMART tunnel during a moderate storm

c. the SMART tunnel during a serious storm

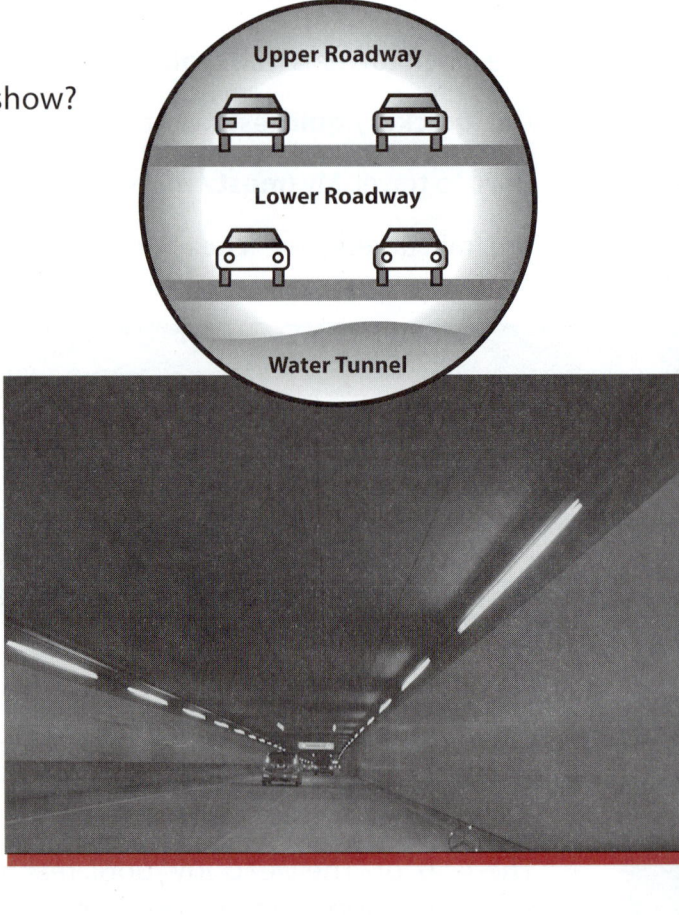

BUILDING SMART

Kuala Lumpur has one of the most innovative tunnels in the world—a combined motorway and stormwater tunnel. It's the longest multi-purpose tunnel in the world.

Malaysia's busy capital city of Kuala Lumpur frequently experiences heavy rains. In the past, these rains have caused serious flooding in the city center, with the rainwater remaining for up to six hours. The floodwaters have damaged property and slowed traffic in the city, resulting in the loss of billions of dollars. To help improve the situation, the government approved the construction of an innovative tunnel—the SMART tunnel.

SMART stands for Stormwater Management and Road Tunnel. Construction began in 2003 and was completed in 2007. Over 30,000 motorists use it every day. The tunnel, which cost about half a billion dollars to build, consists of three sections. The upper two sections are roadways. Each allows traffic to move in one direction. The third, lower section, is a stormwater tunnel. When there is little or no rainfall, the roadway sections are open to motorists and the storm tunnel is closed.

The SMART system is activated during a moderate storm. The floodwater is directed into the lowest section of the tunnel. The upper sections remain open to traffic. However, during a serious storm, both of the two upper roadways become closed to traffic. After all of the vehicles have left the tunnel, gates are opened to allow the floodwaters into the upper sections. All three channels can then carry the floodwaters away from the city center. Within four days, the entire tunnel is opened to traffic again.

Since its opening, the SMART tunnel has prevented many serious floods from affecting Kuala Lumpur. In fact, a huge storm hit the city only three weeks after the SMART tunnel was completed.

B **Read the article.** Circle **T** for True, **F** for False, or **NG** for Not Given.

1. Flooding used to slow down traffic in Kuala Lumpur.   **T   F   NG**

2. It took over 10 years to build the SMART tunnel.   **T   F   NG**

3. During a moderate storm, the top sections of the tunnel stay open to traffic.   **T   F   NG**

4. During a serious storm, the upper sections of the tunnel allow traffic   **T   F   NG**
   in both directions.

5. There are plans to build SMART tunnels in other cities in Malaysia.   **T   F   NG**

Writing

WRITING TIP **Organizing ideas in a chart**

Putting information in a chart can help you see how ideas relate to each other, and help you decide how to organize information.

A **Look at these notes.** Add the key information to the chart.

London, England	also known as 30 St. Mary Axe
unique, modern design	in financial district
mainly an office building	looks like a cucumber
nicknamed the Gherkin	headquarters of large companies

Name	
Location	
Appearance	
What it is	

B **Write a paragraph.** Create a similar chart for a structure you know. Then compare your structure to the Gherkin.

IN CLASS Share your paragraphs.

HE'S A GREAT DIRECTOR, ISN'T HE?

Vocabulary Focus

A **Complete the chart.** Use the words in the box.

clever	stunning	spectacular	brilliant	incredible	overrated
dull	gorgeous	unrealistic	superb	original	predictable

Positive words	Negative words

B **Match.** Join the words to the correct definitions.

1. story   ○   ○ a. clothes worn by actors

2. acting   ○   ○ b. the person an actor plays

3. special effects ○   ○ c. what happens in a book, TV show, or film

4. costumes   ○   ○ d. the music for a film

5. makeup   ○   ○ e. illusions created for film using camerawork or computer graphics

6. soundtrack   ○   ○ f. pretending to be someone on stage or on camera

7. character   ○   ○ g. cosmetics put on an actor's face

Conversation

Complete the conversation. Circle the correct answers.
IN CLASS Practice with a partner.

Marcy: So how did you like the movie?

Jesse: Oh, I loved it. I thought the acting was 1. (**spectacular** / **overrated**). And the 2. (**costumes** / **songs**) were gorgeous. It must have taken a long time to make them.

Marcy: I agree. The acting was 3. (**poor** / **superb**)!

Jesse: And I thought the story was pretty 4. (**predictable** / **original**). I've never seen a movie like that before.

Marcy: Yeah, but I thought the story was pretty 5. (**realistic** / **unrealistic**). That could never happen.

Jesse: What else did you like about the movie?

Marcy: I liked the 6. (**songs** / **special effects**). I'm definitely buying the soundtrack!

Language Focus

A **Match.** Join the questions and answers.

1. You haven't been to England, have you?   ○   ○ a. Yes, it is. Let's leave.

2. That test was pretty hard, wasn't it?   ○   ○ b. No, I didn't go this year.

3. This party is quite boring, isn't it?   ○   ○ c. Yes, he does.

4. Matteo will play for their team, won't he?   ○   ○ d. Yeah, it really was.

5. You didn't go to soccer camp, did you?   ○   ○ e. Actually, I have.

6. Your dad works at the museum, doesn't he? ○   ○ f. No, he won't.

B **Complete the sentences.**

1. The movie was a bit disappointing, _____?

2. You've never been to a movie studio, _____?

3. They can't go backstage without a pass, _____?

4. He _____ seen the sequel yet, has he?

5. They _____ going to see a movie tomorrow, are they?

The Real World

A **Skim the article.** *Spider-Man 2* made $782 million at the box office. Was the film a success or a flop? _____

Movie Budgets

Movies are expensive to make. We often hear of movies with budgets ranging from tens or even hundreds of millions of dollars. Some of the costs come from having a movie with famous actors, or from filming in many locations. But there are also costs that people don't usually know about, such as the cost of music, or getting the rights to the script of a movie. All these costs can add up to a huge amount of money in a movie's production budget.

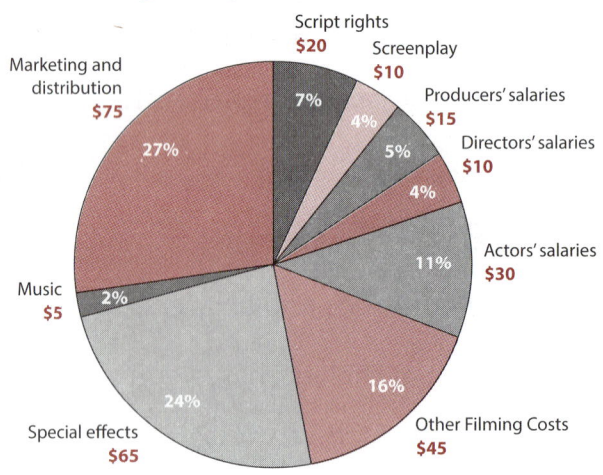

Total budget for *Spider-Man 2*: $275 million

- Script rights $20
- Screenplay $10
- Producers' salaries $15
- Directors' salaries $10
- Actors' salaries $30
- Other Filming Costs $45
- Special effects $65
- Music $5
- Marketing and distribution $75

7%, 4%, 5%, 4%, 11%, 16%, 24%, 2%, 27%

Cost (million US dollars)

But a movie's production budget doesn't tell the whole story. The marketing and distribution of a movie are very important, and movie companies sometimes spend large sums of money here. For the movie *Spider-Man 2*, for example, marketing and distribution cost $75 million. The movie needed to bring in more than $275 million before the company started making any money.

Movies don't always divide up their budget in the same way as the one in the chart. *Spider-Man 2*—an action movie—probably needed more money for special effects. However, for all movies, there is a range of costs—and not all of them are obvious.

B **Read the article.** Circle **T** for True or **F** for False.

1. Movies are expensive to make mainly because actors' salaries are high. **T** **F**

2. The production budget is the entire cost of making a movie. **T** **F**

3. The greatest cost in *Spider-Man 2*'s production budget was special effects. **T** **F**

4. A horror movie is likely to spend more on special effects than a romance film. **T** **F**

Reading

ACTORS IN **VIDEO GAMES**

Video games are a huge part of our culture today. According to the Entertainment Software Association, 59 percent of people in the U.S. played video games in 2013. Video gamers spent over $20 billion on video games that year. This is double the amount the film industry earned in the same year. The game *Grand Theft Auto V* made $1 billion in just three days; no movie does that. The game *Call of Duty: Black Ops* also made over $1 billion.

As games like these regularly make more than Hollywood blockbusters, more and more movie stars are beginning to realize the potential the industry holds for them. Many movie stars are becoming involved in the video game industry in different ways.

A boxer wearing a suit for recording motion capture

One common way is for an actor to lend his or her voice to a video game character. Elijah Wood, who played Frodo in the *Lord of the Rings* movies, voiced the same character in the video game version of the series. Wood loves the challenge. "You find that the characters are in situations that are not real common and you have to . . . vocally make the character seem like he's going through some pretty intense situations," Wood said.

Another way is to "act" in a video game. Through a technique called motion capture, game designers can create a character that looks and moves like an actual person. *Assassin's Creed* character Lucy Stillman was created based on actress Kristen Bell. Bell also lent her voice to the character in this popular series.

Some Hollywood scriptwriters have also had some connections with video games. Mark Protosevich, screenwriter of the movie *Thor*, was involved in the initial writing stages of the movie version of the game *Mass Effect*. He found the writing challenging—he had to write a two-hour movie based on a complicated game that was much longer.

Movies and video games have become more closely connected, and they share many similarities: complicated plots, unique characters, and thrilling action. The popularity of video games is likely to continue, so keep an eye out—or an ear—for your favorite actor the next time you play a video game.

A **Read the article.** Circle the correct answers.

1. Detail According to the article, video games sometimes _____ than Hollywood movies.

   a. are produced faster   b. make more money   c. attract more people

2. **Inference** Wood thinks voicing a video game character is challenging because he has to _____.

    a. be less emotional   b. read more lines   c. react to unusual situations

3. **Detail** Game designers use motion capture to create characters by recording a person's _____.

    a. movement   b. voice   c. thoughts

4. **Inference** One difficulty Protosevich faced in writing a movie version of *Mass Effect* was _____.

    a. creating the characters   b. creating an ending   c. condensing the story

B **Check (✓) the sentences the author would probably agree with.**

1. _____ A video game needs a famous actor to be successful.

2. _____ Video games will continue to be popular.

3. _____ Many movie actors are doing voice acting to improve their acting skills.

4. _____ Working in the video game industry offers different challenges than working in the film industry.

Writing

WRITING TIP Dashes, semicolons, and colons

Be sure to use correct punctuation in your writing, including dashes (—), semicolons (;), and colons (:).

1. Use a **dash** to set off or emphasize information.

    The popularity of video games is likely to continue, so keep an eye out—or an ear—for your favorite actor the next time you play a video game.

2. Use a **semicolon** to separate two related sentences.

    The game *Grand Theft Auto V* made $1 billion in just three days; no movie does that.

3. Use a **colon** before a list.

    Movies and video games have become more closely connected, and they share many similarities: complicated plots, unique characters, and thrilling action.

A **Choose a video game you know.** Take notes using the ideas in the box.

name	characters	who would enjoy it	challenges	three best things about it
how to play it	graphics	things to improve	sound	overall rating (1–5)

B **Use your notes to write a review of the game.** Use correct punctuation.

IN CLASS Share your reviews.

10   I WISH I COULD BE AN ATHLETE!

Vocabulary Focus

A   **Write.** Complete the crossword puzzle.

Across

4. Imagine you can read people's _____. What would you do with that power?

5. Would you ever want to make yourself _____ so no one could see you?

7. Would you want to live _____?

8. Would you rather travel forward or backward in _____?

9. Which _____ would be more fun to have—the ability to fly or to read people's thoughts?

Down

1. If you had the ability to breathe _____, what would you want to do?

2. If you could talk to _____, what questions would you ask them?

3. If you could cure any _____, which one would you choose?

6. If you could speak any _____, which one would you choose?

7. If you could predict the _____, would you want to? Why or why not?

B   **Complete the phrases.** Circle the correct answers.

1. (**speak** / **talk**) a language
2. (**read** / **predict**) the future
3. (**cure** / **repair**) a disease
4. (**turn** / **travel**) backward in time
5. (**set** / **fix**) a world record
6. (**do** / **make**) a wish

C   **IN CLASS**   Ask and answer the questions in **A** with a partner.

Conversation

Complete the conversation. Put the sentences in the correct order.
IN CLASS Practice with a partner.

a. _____ I think it'd be useful for studying cultures around the world.

b. _____ Well, I'm afraid of heights. I think I'd rather have the ability to speak every language.

c. _1_ Hey, Lisa, if you could have a superpower, what would it be?

d. _____ Let's see. . . If I could have any superpower, I'd want to fly. It'd be great to be able to go anywhere in the world.

e. _____ Every language in the world? Why?

Language Focus

A **Complete the sentences.** Circle the correct answers.

1. A: What would you do if you (**could** / **would**) fly? Where would you go?

   B: I'd fly to Egypt. (**I've** / **I'd**) always wanted to visit the pyramids.

2. A: If you could have one wish, what (**should** / **would**) it be?

   B: I'd definitely wish I were (**tallest** / **taller**)!

3. A: If you (**was** / **were**) able to control people's minds, what would you do?

   B: I'd get people to be (**kinder** / **kindest**) to one another!

B **Correct the mistake in each question.** Then match the questions to the correct answers below.

1. _____ If you are a time traveler, which time period would you go back to?

2. _____ If you inventing a robot, what would it do?

3. _____ If you could giving your mother any present, what would it be?

4. _____ If you could be an architect or a lawyer, which should you be?

5. _____ What do you wish you can do very well?

a. I think I'd love designing interesting buildings for people to live in.

b. I wish I could dance well. I'd like to be a professional dancer.

c. I'd probably go back to ancient Egypt.

d. It would help doctors with complicated surgeries.

e. I think a new house would be the perfect gift.

The Real World

A **Skim the article.** Which wishing traditions do the phrases describe? Circle **WW** for Wishing Wells, **BC** for Birthday Candles, or **B** for Both.

1. involves food offerings	**WW**	**BC**	**B**
2. involves money offerings	**WW**	**BC**	**B**
3. was started by ancient Greeks	**WW**	**BC**	**B**
4. is still practiced today	**WW**	**BC**	**B**

Wishing Traditions

Have you ever been told to "make a wish"? Have you ever wondered where these wishing traditions come from?

Wishing Wells

Early European tribes believed that spirits lived in wells. This was because wells held water, an important resource then. Water was thought to have healing powers. People used to go to the wells to pray and ask for help. Some believed that the spirits would grant them their wish if they paid a price, so they would often drop coins into the well. This wishing tradition continues today—people still throw coins into water to make a wish. A famous place to make wishes is the Trevi Fountain in Rome, Italy.

Birthday Candles

Another popular wishing tradition is the blowing out of candles. This may have been started by the ancient Greeks, who made offerings of baked goods to Artemis, the goddess of the moon. The ancient Greeks added candles to the baked goods to represent moonlight. It was believed that the smoke carried people's prayers to the gods. Nowadays, people make a silent wish before blowing out birthday candles.

B **Read the article.** Circle **T** for True or **F** for False.

1. The tradition of wishing wells started in South America.	**T**	**F**
2. People believed spirits lived in wells because these places contained water.	**T**	**F**
3. Candles were used to represent sunlight.	**T**	**F**
4. The ancient Greeks believed that the candle smoke could send their wishes to the gods.	**T**	**F**

Reading

A **Skim the article.** The purpose of the article is to explain _____ .

    a. how crowdsourcing helps grant wishes   b. changes in social media   c. Crowdwish's achievements

MAKING REAL
WISHES COME TRUE

Forget tossing a coin into a wishing well. One company is counting on the power of crowds to make wishes come true.

Crowdwish.com offers users the chance to make wishes. People can wish for anything—products, experiences, money for a cause—with the most popular wish being granted each day. "I know this sounds completely ridiculous," says Bill Griffin, the founder of Crowdwish, "but I wanted to create a site where people could come and ask for literally anything, and get a meaningful and freshly generated response."

A boy's wish gets granted.

How exactly does it work? People can make up to ten wishes per day for anything they want. Users search the wishes already on the site and add their support to these existing wishes, or create new ones. They then gather support for their wishes through social media. The more people who click "me too," the more likely it is that these wishes will be granted. Every 24 hours, the Crowdwish team of negotiators, researchers, and dealmakers takes the most popular wish and does its best to make the wish come true.

Some of the most popular wishes so far have included: providing aid to someone with huge medical bills, creating anti-bullying stickers for schoolchildren, helping people start businesses, and making donations to organizations like the Red Cross.

What happens when Crowdwish can't grant a wish? One user, for example, asked for a life without stress. When that happens, Griffin and his team get creative. In this case, they sent packs of gum to help the wisher relax. "What we do doesn't have to be huge," says Griffin. "I'm happy with the subtle ways we grant wishes." Griffin's ultimate goal is for people to use the website as a force for good. But it doesn't stop someone from asking for a new phone or a vacation in Hawaii.

B **Read the article.** Circle the correct answers.

1. Main Idea Which wish is Crowdwish likely to grant?

    a. the wish with the most support

    b. the first wish of each day

    c. the wish that can help the most people

2. **Detail** Which of the following is true about Crowdwish?

   a. It grants all wishes.   b. Anyone can make a wish.   c. You can make one wish a day.

3. **Detail** Which is NOT given as an example of a wish that Crowdwish granted?

   a. building a school

   b. providing help with medical bills

   c. donating money to charity

4. **Vocabulary** Another word for "subtle" is _____ .

   a. quick   b. honest   c. indirect

Writing

WRITING TIP **Using a variety of sentence structures**

Use sentences of different lengths, types, or structures to add more variety to your writing.

1. Use sentences of different lengths.

   I closed my eyes tightly as I tossed the coin into the well, and then opened them to see if my wish had come true. It had.

2. Use both active and passive sentences.

   I picked the tiny four-leaf clover in the field near my house. I was told a four-leaf clover brought good luck. I put it between the pages of my book.

3. Vary your sentence openers.

   At ten o'clock that night, my sister and I decided to go outside to look at the stars. Suddenly, we saw a shooting star.

A **Imagine you can make something good happen for the following people.** What would you wish for? Take notes.

> a classmate   a close friend   a family member
> a neighbor   your community   your country

I wish I had enough money to take my parents on a nice vacation.

B **Write a paragraph.** Give reasons or an explanation for each wish in **A**. Use a variety of sentence structures.

IN CLASS Share your paragraphs.

11

WHAT WOULD YOU DO?

Vocabulary Focus

(A) **Complete the sentences.** Use the phrases in the box.

> broke   cheated   littering   spread a rumor   stole

1. Randi took a pack of gum from a store without paying for it. He _____ it.

2. Zac _____ on his test; he copied his friend's answers.

3. Michi threw the baseball through the window and _____ it.

4. I just saw Joel _____; he dropped a paper cup on the sidewalk.

5. Kyle _____ about Jesse, even though it's probably not true.

(B) **Match the situations to the advice.**

1. _____ Francis copied a paragraph from a book for his essay.

2. _____ Lily borrowed my book but then lost it.

3. _____ Beth stepped in front of someone who was waiting to get tickets for a movie.

4. _____ Fareed broke his mother's favorite mug.

a. He should apologize to her.

b. She should buy you a new one.

c. She should wait in line like everyone else.

d. He should rewrite it and cite the source.

C **Rank each person's action in A.** Mark them from **1** (most serious) to **5** (least serious).
IN CLASS Compare with a partner.

Randi	Zac	Michi	Joel	Kyle

Conversation

Correct five mistakes in the conversation.
IN CLASS Practice with a partner.

Wes: Hey! Where's my cake? I put it in the fridge last night, and now it's gone.

Maria: I have no idea. Maybe someone was eaten it.

Wes: Who would do that? I've been looked forward to eating that cake all day.

Maria: You could asked the people in the office. Maybe someone will admit they took it.

Wes: I guess. Hey, I just remembered! Today's Friday. The fridge cleaned out every
         Thursday night. It was probably just thrown into the trash. What a waste!

Maria: Yeah, you're probably right. Maybe you would label your food next time.

Wes: I think that's what I'll do.

Language Focus

A **Complete the sentences.** Use the correct forms of the words in parentheses.

1. He's _____ (**wait**) in line for five hours.

2. My uncle _____ (**take**) to the hospital last night.

3. The children _____ (**watch**) cartoons all day long.

4. This building _____ (**design**) a famous architect.

5. These houses _____ (**paint**) last year.

B **Complete the sentences.** Circle the correct answers.

1. You (**shouldn't** / **should have** / **shouldn't have**) talk in the library.

2. If I (**see** / **saw** / **was seen**) a crime, I'd call the police.

3. My wallet (**steal** / **was stolen** / **has been stealing**) from my backpack.

4. My homework isn't in my bag. I (**might** / **must have** / **should have**) left it at home.

5. They've been (**play** / **was played** / **playing**) their music loudly recently.

6. He (**must** / **must have** / **couldn't have**) broken it. He wasn't there.

A **Skim the article.** What is an alternative title for the article?

a. The Benefits of Piracy

b. Piracy—A Profitable Business

c. The Growing Problem of Online Piracy

The Hidden Costs of Online Piracy

Take this short quiz.

	Yes	No
• Have you downloaded music from the Internet without paying for it?	○	○
• Have you ever copied music and given it to your friends?	○	○
• Have you shared or downloaded music or movies from an online file-sharing network?	○	○

If you have answered "yes" to any of the questions above, you may be an online pirate.

Most people know that piracy is a crime, so why do they still do it? Most pirated CDs and DVDs sold on the street cost as little as 20 percent of the original price. If you download a movie or music from a file-sharing network, it's free. And it's easy. Online piracy is quick, and the files are instantly available. And if nobody gets hurt, is it really a crime?

It's easy to think that piracy doesn't hurt anyone. You may think that illegally downloading one song or movie isn't that big a deal. But when millions of people around the world do it, it causes serious harm to the owners of the music or movie—they do not receive any income from pirated goods. But the impact of piracy is wider than that. A recent study on music piracy reported that the damage to the industry results in more than 70,000 lost job opportunities and $2 billion in lost wages to American workers each year.

Piracy is a serious problem in many countries, and several laws have been put in place to counter this problem. A lawsuit could cost you thousands of dollars. In the U.S., you could be jailed and/or fined. Other countries also have their own laws against piracy. So the next time you're thinking of downloading something illegally, think of the people who will be affected by your actions, and don't get yourself in trouble. Don't be an online pirate.

B **Read the article.** Circle **T** for True or **F** for False.

1. It's illegal to share and distribute a song that you created.   T   F

2. Online piracy is quick, easy, and usually free.   T   F

3. For each pirated song or movie, the owner receives 20% of the profits.   T   F

4. Piracy is a problem all over the world.   T   F

5. You could face jail time for online piracy.   T   F

Reading

A **Skim the article.** What is the most suitable title for this reading?

    a. Is It OK to Lie?   b. Lying Is Wrong   c. The Truth Hurts

We all lie. Despite the fact that we've been taught that lying is wrong, everyone has lied at some point in their lives. But is lying really always wrong?

Consider this situation: Your grandmother sends you a sweater for your birthday. You hate the color, but thank her anyway, and promise to wear it often. Or imagine you go to a friend's birthday party. The food her mother prepared doesn't taste good. If she asks you if you enjoyed your meal, you don't want to offend her, so you say, "Yes, it was great." We call these lies "white lies"—lies that are seemingly innocent and do no harm. We lie to protect the feelings of others or to make them feel good about themselves.

However, are there situations where lying is necessary? Imagine this: You have been late to school every day for a week. Your teacher has threatened to suspend you if you're late again. Despite setting your alarm for an earlier time, you are still late. Your only hope of not being suspended is to lie and say that your bus broke down on the way to school. Would you lie, or tell the truth and accept the consequences? Now, imagine something more serious: You're in a supermarket and a frantic young man runs by you and hides in a corner. Seconds later, an angry-looking person with a knife comes in asking if you've seen a young man run past. What would you do? If you tell the truth, the young man may get hurt. Lying may in fact save his life.

On the other hand, consider the birthday party scenario again. Telling your friend's mother a lie does not help her improve her cooking. She's likely to serve the same bad food in the future. So the question remains: Is it OK to lie or not?

B **Read the article.** Circle the correct answers.

1. Detail What is a "white lie"?

    a. a harmless lie   b. a lie to cheat someone   c. a lie meant to cause harm

2. Inference According to the article, lying is sometimes necessary in order to _____.

    a. help someone improve

    b. find out the truth

    c. prevent bad consequences

3. Vocabulary The word "frantic" can be replaced with _____.

    a. sad   b. anxious   c. shocked

4. Inference Which of these statements would the author most likely agree with?

  a. People who often lie can't form good relationships with others.

  b. A lie can be bad or helpful depending on the situation.

  c. Telling the truth is the best way to deal with any situation.

C **Have you been in a situation where you had to lie for a good reason?**
   IN CLASS Share your experience with a partner.

Writing

WRITING TIP **Using persuasive language**

Use persuasive language to make your opinion or argument stronger. Look at these phrases.

I strongly believe (that) . . .	**Clearly, / Obviously, / Surely, . . .**
Of course, . . .	**I'm sure / certain (that) . . .**
Without a doubt, . . .	**From my point of view, . . .**

A **Circle the choice that expresses your opinion.**

1. It's (**sometimes / never**) OK to search someone's phone history.

2. Stealing food is (**acceptable if / unacceptable even if**) you are starving.

3. It's best to (**avoid saying anything hurtful / be honest**) when settling an argument between two friends.

4. You should pursue a career in the field you (**are best at / have the most passion for**).

5. If someone cheats on an exam, they should (**fail the class / be suspended from school**).

B **Choose one statement from A.** List three reasons to support your opinion.

C **Write a paragraph expressing your opinion.** Use persuasive language to make your argument stronger.

   IN CLASS Share your paragraph with someone who has an opposite opinion.

12

YOU SHOULD EAT MORE FRUIT!

Vocabulary Focus

A **Complete the sentences.** Circle the correct answers.

1. Brown rice and barley are examples of (**sugars** / **whole grains**).

2. A balanced diet means eating (**different foods** / **red meat**) in the right amounts.

3. Meat is a good source of (**salt** / **protein**), but it is better to eat less red meat and more nuts and tofu.

4. Too much (**water** / **sugar**) can cause weight problems and diabetes.

5. Healthy (**fats** / **caffeine**) can be good for your heart.

6. (**Caffeine** / **Protein**) can be found in coffee, soda, and black tea.

7. (**Soda** / **Water**) is the best drink for your body.

B **Complete the sentences.** Use the words in the box.

> exercise   healthy   nap   sugar   red   whole

1. Try to eat _____ fats like olive oil.

2. It's best to _____ regularly to maintain a healthy body weight.

3. It's OK to eat _____ meat, but eat it in moderation.

4. Eating less _____ can help you lose weight.

5. You should eat _____ grains like brown rice.

6. If you need to take a(n) _____ in the middle of the day, do it.

Conversation

Complete the conversation. Circle the correct answers.

IN CLASS Practice with a partner.

Ari: Hey, Matt, let's go for a walk.

Matt: I'm sorry, Ari. I 1. (**can't** / **don't**) feel like going for a walk today. I'm too tired.

Ari: You don't look so good. You didn't get much sleep last night, 2. (**did** / **didn't**) you?

Matt: No, I didn't. I was up all night playing video games with my brother.

Ari: You know, 3. (**play** / **playing**) video games is fine, but you really 4. (**should** / **would**) take better care of yourself. You hardly eat any 5. (**fruit and vegetables** / **sugar and caffeine**). And you don't get much exercise, either.

Matt: You're right, Ari. You're 6. (**fitter** / **fatter**) than me. What kind of exercise would you suggest?

Ari: 7. (**Swim** / **Swimming**) is a great exercise. It burns a lot of calories and helps build strength.

Language Focus

A **Correct one mistake in each sentence.**

1. Eat less sugar can help you lose weight.

2. Lean meat—like chicken and turkey—is more healthy than red meat.

3. My sister, Louisa, is the fitter person I know.

4. Vegetables are good for you, don't they?

5. I'm not enough fit to run two kilometers.

6. My doctor, which helped me improve my diet, also suggested I join a gym.

B **Complete the sentences.** Circle the correct answers.

1. Whole grains are (**as healthy** / **healthier**) than processed grains.

2. This coffee is not (**hot enough** / **hottest**).

3. (**Exercising** / **Exercise**) is a great way to relax.

4. Yogurt, (**which** / **who**) has a lot of calcium, is good for you.

5. Mental exercise is (**most important** / **as important as**) physical exercise.

6. Natalie, (**which** / **who**) loves sports, plays badminton every week.

The Real World

A **Skim the article.** Check (✓) the topics that are mentioned in the reading.

1. _____ the first cup of tea

2. _____ who took tea to Europe

3. _____ how tea helped factory workers

4. _____ how tea is grown

5. _____ different types of tea

6. _____ how tea kept people healthy

Tea is a big part of British culture. In fact, tea has played a very important role in many cultures. China is considered to have the longest history of tea drinking—records date back to the 10th-century B.C. In 1606, tea was brought to Europe by Dutch traders. From there, it spread throughout Europe and eventually reached Britain.

Between the 1700s and 1800s, Britain underwent the Industrial Revolution. Instead of farming the land, people now worked in manufacturing. Tea provided some of the fuel for this revolution. During this period, many people worked in factories. However, work was often boring, dangerous, and tiring. Factory workers would drink tea during their breaks. The caffeine in tea, combined with the sugary snacks that were eaten during the break, gave workers the boost they needed to complete the day's work.

The most important, yet often overlooked, benefit of tea was its ability to prevent outbreaks of diseases during this time. The process of boiling water to prepare tea killed bacteria and prevented many deadly diseases from spreading. As a result, the workforce remained strong, and workers were always available for work in factories.

Tea shaped the history of Britain, and is still an important part of its culture today.

B **Read the article.** Circle the correct answers.

1. How long have people been drinking tea?

   a. since the 10th-century B.C.   b. since 1606   c. since the 1700s

2. Tea was brought to Europe by _____.

   a. Chinese traders   b. Dutch traders   c. British factory workers

3. To "overlook" something means to _____ something.

   a. think too much about   b. observe   c. leave out

4. How did tea help during the Industrial Revolution?

   a. It helped workers work longer hours and kept people healthy.

   b. Growing tea created jobs for farmers.

   c. Tea breaks allowed workers to rest.

Reading

A **Skim the article.** Write the letters of the subheadings in the correct places.

    a. Use Your Senses   b. Find Shortcuts   c. Classify Information   d. Link Ideas

HOW TO IMPROVE YOUR MEMORY

The brain is not a computer. If it were, we'd never forget anything. But we do. Memory is a complicated process. Remembering information is not easy to do, but there are ways to improve your memory.

1. _____ Your mind is like a filing system. We find it easier to remember information when it is grouped or organized. If you are going shopping, for example, organize your list in your mind, perhaps by grouping the meat, vegetables, and dairy items separately.

2. _____ To use association, create a visual in your mind. This can help you remember something else. When you think of the image, you can think of the piece of information you assigned to it. For example, if you can't remember your student ID number—487710—try this: Maybe 48 is your house number, 7 is your favorite soccer player Ronaldo's jersey number (twice), and you have 10 toes. Picture yourself at your front door greeting Ronaldo, but he steps on your 10 toes. The more unique the image, the easier it will be to remember.

3. _____ You can stimulate more of your brain if you involve your other senses when trying to memorize information. When more of your brain is activated, it may help you remember better. Writing out your notes while saying them aloud is one well-known study trick. Tapping your toes can help you remember songs or dialogs.

4. _____ Acronyms and acrostics are shortcuts to remembering. An acronym is a word formed by the first letters of other words. The name "Roy G. Biv" helps you remember a rainbow's colors: red, orange, yellow, green, blue, indigo, and violet. Acrostics are similar to acronyms, but in a sentence. To remember the clockwise order on a compass, just think of "Never Eat Sour Watermelons" (north, east, south, west).

There are many other ways that we can memorize information. By making our brain do these "mental workouts," we can make it better at storing and recalling information, and keep it healthy.

B **Match.** Join each situation to the memorization method used.

1. To remember a poem, Claudia sings it and acts it out in front of a mirror. ○   ○ a. association

2. To remember the order of the planets, Sam memorizes the sentence *My very educated mother just served us noodles.* ○   ○ b. an acrostic

3. To remember the conjunctions *for, and, nor, but, or, yet,* and *so,* Bernadette remembers the word *fanboys.* ○   ○ c. using the senses

4. To remember that the capital of Bulgaria is the city of Sofia, Jay pictures a bull named Gary, wearing a cap while sitting on a sofa. ○   ○ d. organization

5. To help her remember her errands, Carol divides them into things to do before lunch and things to do after. ○   ○ e. an acronym

Writing

WRITING TIP **Using similes and metaphors**

Use similes or metaphors in your writing to create a vivid image in the reader's mind. A simile compares things using **like** or **as**, while a metaphor says that one thing **is** something else.

Similes
My friend and I are **like** two peas in a pod.
The examination hall was **as** silent **as** a grave.

Metaphors
The ground **was** a blanket of snow.
The clear waters of the river **are** a mirror.

A **Read the sentences.** Then circle **S** for simile or **M** for metaphor.

1. Time is money.   S   M

2. She couldn't believe her eyes—it was like a dream.   S   M

3. His heart is made of stone.   S   M

4. Jack and Harry are twins, but they're as different as night and day.   S   M

B **Write a paragraph.** Describe how to achieve healthy skin, a healthy brain, or a healthy heart. Include a simile or metaphor.

C **IN CLASS** **Share your paragraph with a partner.** Do you agree with each other's ideas and suggestions?

Photo Credits

1 Massimo Borchi/Atlantide Phototravel/Corbis, **3** mbbirdy/Getty Images, **4** vi mart/Shutterstock, **6** Janie Airey/cultura/Corbis, **9** (t) AP Photo/Muhammed Muheisen, **11** Ahturner/Shutterstock, **12** Jerod Harris/FilmMagic/Getty Images, **14** Justin Paget/Crave/Corbis, **17** sturti/E+/Getty Images, **19** Joel Sartore/NGC, **21** Joel Sartore/NGC, **22** (t) Marilyn Gould/Dreamstime, (b) Peter Hermes Furian/Shutterstock, **24** (t) Jeff Vanuga/Flirt/Corbis, (cl) elnavegante/Shutterstock, (c) Mario Verin/SOPA RF/Ramble/Corbis, (cr) I Love Travel/Shutterstock, **26** Yasuhito Izuki, **27** Tony Waltham/Robert Harding World Imagery/Corbis, **29** Linda Bucklin/Shutterstock, **31** AP/Wide World Photos, **32** AP Photo/Roberto Borea, **34** Julian Kaesler/Getty Images, **36** Andrey Burmakin/Shutterstock, **37** Ira Block/NGC, **39** (t) Noppasin/Shutterstock, **40** Geoffrey Kirman/Alamy, **41** Solent News/Splash News/Newscom, **42** Dr. Sayid Budi, **44** Nathan Jones/Getty Images, **46** (bkg) AF archive/Alamy, **47** Jeff Vinnick/Getty Images, **49** imagemaker/Shutterstock, **51** Blend Images/Shutterstock, **52** Bill Wippert/Getty Images, **54** Simone Becchetti/E+/Getty Images, **56** Pedro Lobo/Bloomberg/Getty Images, **57** Sean Justice/The Image Bank/Getty Images, **59** Aleksandar Mijatovic/Shutterstock, **61** Lenetstan/Shutterstock, **62** PathDoc/Shutterstock

NGC = National Geographic Creative

Art Credits

9 (cr) Leremy/Shutterstock, (cr) Francesco Abrignani/Shutterstock, (cr) (cl) bioraven/Shutterstock, (cr) Macrovector/Shutterstock, (cr) (cl) Snorks/Shutterstock, (cl) SoleilC/Shutterstock, (cl) Mushakesa/Shutterstock, **30** Gaim Creative Studio, **39** (cl) bioraven/Shutterstock, (cl) (cr) Leremy/Shutterstock, (cl) (cr) Vladgrin/Shutterstock, (cl) angelh/Shutterstock, (cr) iconerinfostock/Shutterstock